Writing & I
Christian Music

God's Plan & Purpose for the Church

Peter Lawrence Alexander

Follow *Me!* Books
An imprint of Alexander Publishing
PO Box 1720, Petersburg, VA 23805

Writing and Performing Christian Music

Follow *Me!* Books
An Imprint of Alexander Publishing
a division of Alexander University, Inc.
P.O. Box 1720, Petersburg, VA, 23805
www.alexanderpublishing.com

Paperback edition published 2007
ISBN: 978-0-939067-77-0

Printed in the United States of America

Interior design by Caroline J. Alexander
Cover design by Caroline J. Alexander

Alexander, Peter Lawrence, 1950-

Lord, this one's for you.

...

CONTENTS

Foreword

Robert Kral

Christian Music. What do these words mean to you? For some it's a sense of relief of being assured the music won't offend, that it will lift God's name and lift our souls toward heaven. For others it might be a source of cringing, however, as with different eyes and ears we might be aware of a misuse of music in Churches today where worship is far less than what it needs to be. I'm reminded of how Jesus used the imagery of sheep: That we are sheep that are following and being shepherded by Christ. Yet, have many of us not become sheep that are merely following each other, rather than Christ?

In this sense, do we attend Church services following each other, blindly singing our way through worship without understanding what it is we are doing? What is true worship and what really is the function, now and in history, of the music that the Church makes so much use of? Are we using music as it was intended by God?

Music to be sure, is a powerful gift from God. In song we express so much of what we find hard to express, thanks to the words and music God has gifted us with. If this music and lyric indeed comes from God, and is offered in worship to him, should we not understand completely what this means, what God's intention for music in worship should be, and how we might stray from what true worship really is?

I think it's all too easy to follow each other, to be sheep that have gone astray following each other or the "norm" rather than sheep that follow and know our Master's voice. In understanding the origins of music in worship, we come back to what it means to truly worship and honor our Lord.

In reading the work and writings here of Peter Alexander, you'll come to a clear understanding of these origins and intentions of music in worship. May God enlighten you with the results of this research, that you may know and understand with clarity how music, that which speaks for us what is often so hard for us to express ourselves, might be likened to the Holy Spirit as it moves us and elevates our souls closer to God. We're to follow our Master's voice, and so in reading this study may you come closer to Him, with new understanding as to what it means to make the right use of this that He has given us: The gift of music.

ROBERT KRAL
MAY 24TH, 2007

Composer for *Angel, Miracles,* and *Superman: Doomsday*

INTRODUCTION

DR. WILLIAM L. HOOPER

There are many people who have a deep relationship with Christ who want to express that relationship by writing songs. How do they go about it? Who or what is the model they should follow? Where do they start? Should they use certain sounds, instruments, styles and rhythms because these are "Christian"?

It must be frustrating to these fledgling songwriters to see soloists and groups with tours and recording contracts dominate the contemporary Christian music scene. Song writing is driven by commercial interests where a song is good if it is popular and profitable. How can they possibly write songs of that stature?

It must be frustrating, too, that the current atmosphere in many churches and denominations can lead the potential songwriter to believe that songs must use certain sounds, rhythms, styles and instruments if they are to be acceptable. Songs of personal faith that are written and performed in a way that his or her church finds objectionable are forbidden and the songwriter is isolated.

Peter Alexander takes the position that there are biblical principles to guide the songwriter in writing his or her songs. These principles are not dependent upon any particular culture, or language or performing medium. These principles are not dependent upon commercial acceptability. Principles are derived from an exegesis of biblical passages that describe the purpose and use of music in both Old and New Testaments.

A very important part of this book is a study of various psalms, their purpose and their textual patterns that can be used as examples to follow in writing one's own songs. The author does not focus on the specifics of how to write a song or how to make a CD or to organize a band. Rather, the emphasis is upon what the Bible says can go into a song!

One important principle is that songs are not written to imitate Christian songs that are currently successful and popular. Nor should songs be written as the first step to a career as a Christian performing artist. The aim should be to write songs that edify the body of Christ.

This book should give encouragement to those who recognize they do not have the abilities and contacts necessary to be a Christian performing artist. Yet, they have a burning desire to express their relationship to Christ through words and/or music. They will discover that they can learn how to write songs that will honor Christ and build up His Body. They will discover that they can learn and develop the natural ability God has given them. They will learn what it takes to be a music leader in their church. The secret is to learn and apply the biblical principles that Peter Alexander shares with them.

DR. WILLIAM L. HOOPER
JUNE 28TH, 2007

Former Dean of the School of Church Music at
New Orleans Baptist Theological Seminary

Professor Emeritus, Southwest Baptist University

AUTHOR
Ministry & Musicians
Church Music in Transition
Music Education in the Church
A Curriculum Guide for Children's Choir
Fundamentals of Music

PREFACE

WHAT *IS* CHRISTIAN MUSIC?

When I was at music school in Boston in the early '70s, I was really frustrated by how I was being taught classical composition and orchestration in my junior and senior years. One afternoon, a question formed in my mind - *how did the great composers teach themselves?* Answering that question has occupied a great deal of my life, but out of that came a curriculum and the foundation for what grew into Alexander Publishing.

A similar situation birthed this book that came out of my devotion time. The first question was, "What's the word *praise* really mean?" That started my research into the Old Testament where I found that there were several words translated *praise*, but they all had different meanings.

The next question was, "Is there a word for *song* in Hebrew?" There is, and it means the same as the word *song* does today in the 21st Century. So as I did my research, I began finding complete songs in the Old Testament and in the Psalms.

Then came the next question: What's the word *psalm* mean? When I found the answer to that question I saw that there was a lot of information in the Bible about setting the Psalms to music that hadn't been passed down to those of us who write and produce Christian music.

Well, by the time I had all these questions answered, two pastors and a worship leader suggested that I organize the material and write a book.

As I reviewed these materials, I sensed the Holy Spirit guiding me to refine the material and address this question, "What *is* Christian music and what, if anything, does the Bible have to say about performing it?"

Out of this series of questions has come this book, *Writing and Performing Christian Music*. It's written *first* for the creators and producers of musical song and composition: songwriters, musicians, worship leaders, vocalists, and composers who want to sing and play to the Lord (regardless of their musical skill level).

After that, it's for church leadership, and then to anyone else involved with producing and airing Christian music including execs at Christian record companies, Christian radio stations and the various Christian television networks.

To "define" what Christian music is, and to present a Biblical foundation on which to answer this question, I've done extensive Biblical research that:

- Exegetes each of the three passages by Paul that describe the use of music in the early church (the *ekklesia*, meaning *the called out ones*, the *assembly*)
- Looks at nearly all the songs in the Old Testament labeled *shi'yr* (Hebrew for *song*)
- Identifies 22 different song types by content in the Bible
- Defines the multiple words translated *praise* and shows which songs go with which word thus creating specific types of Biblical praise songs
- Defines God's purpose with Christian music and how that dovetails with Christ's mission statement in Luke 4:16-21
- Examines specific Hebrew lyric techniques used to create many of the Psalms that can still be used today
- Clarifies why lyric content is more important than style, beat and rhythm
- Gives direction for writing effective Christian songs in any language and any culture
- Defines the Biblical purpose and use of music (which is consistent in both the Old and New Testaments) in helping us be successful in the race each of us is called to run and finish

Here's what all this research says in a single sentence: *what makes a song Christian is the lyric, not the musical style.* As you'll learn, lyrics enter the mind and shape the soul (heart) of an individual. That's why the lyrics we write are incredibly important. Melody, harmony, and rhythm are cultural, therefore transitional. But lyrics, that which shapes the soul, are multi-generational. What shapes me impacts those around me today, and my immediate family generationally. Because the focus is on the content of what makes a song a Christian song, I have not covered specific techniques for pop songwriting. For that musical discussion, I refer you to Sheila Davis' *The Craft of Lyric Writing* and my text *Applied Professional Harmony 101*, which complements Ms. Davis' book.

PERFORMANCE PRACTICES

The Bible has a lot to say about performance practice. When you understand that the word *psalm* in Greek means *plucked* (referring to an instrument today like an acoustic guitar), an arranging/performance imperative arises. It suggests that all the song lyrics in the Psalms were designed to be performed with plectrum instruments along with whatever instruments are written in the instructions to the Chief Musician. Any experienced arranger knows that a plectrum instrument with a solo voice, or several voices, creates intimacy, and also requires the audience to listen quietly and with more focus. To this were added those instruments that supported the lyric.

Across both Testaments, the purpose and use of song is consistent. However, the performance practices changed from a structured environment starting with the Tent of Meeting set by David, to the less structured environment of what today we call the home church as established by Paul.

I cover this in more detail in the section marked *Prelude*, but for now I want to define *church* using the word that Jesus used, and which is used throughout the New Testament - *ekklesia*. It means, *the called out ones*. In Greek, it's also translated as *assembly* which was the ruling governing council in a city. In the Greek version of the Old Testament, called the Septuagint, *ekklesia* is also used to define the Israelites called out of Egypt.

THE KEY WORDS FOR WORSHIP

What are we really talking about when we use the word *worship*?

The Hebrew word *shachah*, means *to bow down*, and is translated *worship* 99 times out of 142 in the King James. Its first use is in Genesis 18:2 (See also Genesis 23:7, 12).

And he lift up his eyes and looked, and, lo, three men stood by him: and when he saw them, he ran to meet them from the tent door, and ***bowed*** *[shachah] himself toward the ground,*

The Greek equivalent is *proskuneo*, which means *to kiss the hand*, or *to fall upon your knees and touch the ground with your forehead*. Looking at Genesis 18:2 in the Septuagint, the word is *proskunetes* where it's translated *obeisance*. *Proskunetes* is first found in John 4:23. Jesus defines worship for us in John 4: 23-24.

But the hour cometh, and now is, when the true ***worshipp****ers [proskunetes] shall* ***worship*** *[proskuneo] the Father in spirit [pneuma] and in truth [aletheia]: for the Father seeketh [zeteo] such to* ***worship*** *[proskuneo] him. God is a Spirit: and they that* ***worship*** *[proskuneo] him must* ***worship*** *[proskuneo] him in spirit [pneuma] and in truth [aletheia].*

Jesus is teaching that God Himself *seeks out* men and women who will bow to Him. And Abraham is our model of what that means. We bow to God with our spirit (*pneuma*) and with a truth that's objective and true in any matter under consideration. We see this action in the last use of *proskuneo* in the New Testament, Revelation 4:10, where the elders fall down to their knees and toss their crowns towards the throne.

Isn't it interesting that in the Old Testament, whether in Hebrew or in Greek with the Septuagint, song leaders are *never* called worship leaders. Song leaders lead and conduct the congregation, they point the congregation to God, but that is as far as it goes. From that point forward, worship, *proskuneo*, comes from me the worshipper, *proskunetes*, from my spirit, *pneuma*, in truth, *aletheia*, with whatever God chooses to reveal to me and calls me to do, including leaving Ur for Canaan.

I worship, *shachah/proskuneo*, when I choose to bow to the Lord, which describes my individual attitude and action of singing to, playing to, and doing all things unto the Lord. Thus, *shachah/proskuneo* is to be a way of life for a Follower of Christ.

Once we understand this, now we're prepared to better understand God's planning and purposing of music within the *ekklesia*, the *called out ones*, the *assembly*.

SINGING TO THE LORD BUILDS TRUST

Phrases talking about *singing to the Lord, singing unto God*, speak to the *relational* aspect of building your relationship with God. This sounds rather theological until you stop and realize that making yourself vulnerable to sing or to play to another person is very intimate. Even if you're tough on the outside, on the inside you're emotionally wide open. Anyone who has ever demoed a song, or auditioned, understands the almost nerve wracking sense of vulnerability you experience before, during, and after! You feel so *vulnerable* unless you really know and trust that other person!

Whether you're an amateur or professional, singing to the Lord is a step in building a trusting relationship with Him. To bow down to God is to become vulnerable.

There's a play by Robert Anderson, later adapted for film, called, *I Never Sang For My Father*. I'm sure that many can relate to that title. But as Christians, we have a heavenly Father who adopted us to whom we *can* sing and who *wants* to listen. With God, there's no performance. No rejection. It's just He and I in my studio, sometimes in my headphones, other times with the monitors on. And I play. Regardless of my skill level, with God, I can say, "I sing to you."

Bowing down to God in spirit and in truth is not singing and playing to an ethereal God who's way out there beyond my reach and comprehension. Rather, it's singing to our *adopted* Father in heaven. At our invitation, our adopted Dad sits with us, and listens to us, as we sing or play to Him.

When I sit and sing or just play to the Lord, I play at whatever performance level I've achieved. I play what comes from my spirit within. My adopted Father, who sits with me, listens to me. This is a tangible way that I as an artist learn that God accepts me, that I don't have to have a performance relationship with Him.

So in the New Testament, when Paul said, *"Someone bring a song,"*[1] I bring what I sing to the Lord at whatever skill level I'm at today, in whatever style (or styles) I can write in. Musically, this is how I bow to Him.

When I sing or write to the Lord, that's my musical offering. And He receives it.

Christian Music Is Local

What I learned by studying the music practices of the *ekklesia* is that Christian music is local. It comes out of the local assembly. And the styles listened to and sung with also come out of the local body.

I believe this has significant theological importance at the local level in light of Acts 17:26 (NIV) where Paul says, *"From one man he made every nation of men, that they should inhabit the whole earth; and he determined the times set for them and the exact places where they should live."*

The Bible is clear that God has planned for us to be in a specific geographic place in a specific time. So the first place our music is to have audience and impact is locally through the local body, provided, of course, the local church is allowing for that. I'll touch more on this in Chapter 8.

[1] I Cor. 14:26

TO BUILD THE BODY

"Is Christian music *only* sung to God?"

From Deuteronomy (God to Moses), Joshua (God to Joshua), and Paul (applying from Moses and Joshua), I discovered that Christian music is something we also sing to ourselves and to each other. From Scripture, we learn that songs are to edify and build the body, to confront, and to have prophetic impact.

Thus, a pattern emerges:

- I sing to God
- I sing to myself
- I sing to others
- We corporately sing to God and to each other

As you read this book and look at the songs in the Bible (presented in the order of their appearance) you're going to discover, as I did, the lyric depth of what we can sing to each other and to God. The songs in the Bible that God has given to build the Body, are models for the lyric content of the new songs we're to write.

LYRICS ANYONE CAN UNDERSTAND...

To have positive impact, lyrics must be easy for people to understand, and that applies equally to those who've committed to following Christ and to those who haven't. When we read the song lyrics in the Bible one thing stands out: except for selected references (some of which are geographic), most anyone can read the lyrics of a song in the Bible and understand immediately what's being said. They may not understand all the references, but the *intent* is certainly clear.

MANY WRITTEN BY A MAN'S MAN

Many of the songs in the Bible were written by a professional soldier who became a statesman. His songs came out of those two periods in his life, a portion of which was also spent as a professional military mercenary. Granted, it's much more idyllic to think of David writing these songs in a lovely field with sheep off to the side. And I'm sure some were. But a more realistic view is that they were written by a professional soldier, who, over a period of years engaged in fierce hand-to-hand combat on the ground and with light cavalry, and who, eye-to-eye, killed other men. At least one song was written during a period when King Saul was literally hunting David down to kill him.

What does it say that God selected a man like David to write over one third of the songs in the Bible?

One thing's for sure when you read David's lyrics [2], especially in a modern translation, is that these songs came out of *real* life, some of which were literally written on the run. What we discover is that David's lyrics are emotionally honest, intense, and at times brutally *frank*. We learn that it's *manly* to write songs to God, and from David, we men (and women, too) learn how to openly express love to God. We also learn a language of emotion.

The "kicker" to all this is that these songs, written by a professional soldier, were performed publicly.

LEADERSHIP IN MUSIC AS SET BY DAVID

No doubt because of his experience with Saul, David knew first hand the power music can have with an individual. I believe that's why David set clear leadership guidelines with job descriptions and duties for those in the Tent of Meeting music department.

Specifically, one leader stands out, Chenaniah. In exegeting the music sections of I Chronicles, I discovered something special about this musical leader.

Chenaniah was a tribal leader (*archon* in Greek) who was appointed the leader of the singers because he possessed *wisdom* (in Hebrew, *bene*). When you do a word study on *bene*, you discover its first use is in Genesis where Pharaoh defined as a "hiring" characteristic, what was needed in the court official who would be assigned by the government to prepare for the coming famine. The second use of that word in Genesis is applied to Joseph who matched Pharaoh's job description.

So, Chenaniah was selected to be the musical director over the singers because he had the kind of skill and wisdom that Joseph had. What this communicates is that God wants leaders in all areas of Christian music. In short, leadership first, then music.

---

[2] According to Dr. Ron Allen, author of, *And I Will Praise Him*, all of the Psalms are song lyrics, not poems, which were written in the style of the day.

Because of this leadership imperative, I've taken the time in Chapter 9 to both list and define the job positions as found in the Tent of Meeting music staff. What you'll discover is that the appointed position of worship leader was handled with striking difference when compared to the present worship leader movement. Worship leaders under David, more accurately described in the texts as song leaders, did *not* have the wide authority that many present day worship leaders do. For some worship leaders, this may be unsettling, but in David's Tent of Meeting, song leaders were rotated and performed under the musical direction of Chenaniah.

I've included this leadership discussion because it's a serious part of both performing Christian music within the *ekklesia* along with determining what should be sung.

LIVE PERFORMANCE CONSIDERATIONS

Finally, I've covered some general live performance considerations, along with some thoughts on selecting music in the contemporary church.

BREAKIN' IN?

In closing, I do feel the need to comment about one aspect of contemporary Christian music that really bothers me, and that's this whole idea of "breakin' in" to the Christian music scene, and that includes some church music departments!

"Breakin' in" is a *career* concern. We do not "break in" at church. In church, it's about the work of service. And that's different. Ideally, the local church music ministry, as we'll see with Paul, should be leading by encouraging and performing new songs and larger works. Out from this comes musical leaders, not stars, and not people seeking a career as Christian music artists, but some of whom God *might* elevate to that position. This is not to say, nor suggest, that having a recording contract, a hit song, or a tour is "wrong." Far from it. But it is to say that, as Paul noted, the purpose of Christian music is to edify the *ekklesia*.

That is our principle concern.

PETER LAWRENCE ALEXANDER
SUMMER 2007
Petersburg, Virginia

AUTHOR'S NOTE

Two days after I wrote the preface, I awoke with the thought that I needed to amplify from the *Preface* that the Psalms were written by *men*.

Whether this thought is from the Holy Spirit or my subconscious, I'll leave for you to decide. But as I pondered this throughout the day, here's what I realized.

That the Psalms were written by men demonstrates the range of emotion a man can possess and express in his spiritual life, and still keep going in the face of overwhelming adversity, as David and others certainly experienced. It shows us that men have emotions, strong emotions, and with God, have the room to express them. Here, through song.

It also means that men who have difficulty in knowing how to safely express their feelings, can come to the Psalms and learn.

At least two of the men who wrote Psalms were experienced in hand-to-hand combat, Moses and David. The Bible doesn't tell us Moses' military record, but the historian Josephus does, and Moses' tactical skill in desert warfare was significant. When we read that David was able to creep up behind Saul in a cave and cut the tassel off his robe and not be caught, this demonstrates a highly trained Special Operations *warrior* at the caliber of the Green Berets, US Navy SEALs, GSG9, SAS, or Marine Force Recon. In short, the *men* who wrote these Psalms were *not* wimps. They were *not* passive. God was *not* their *crutch*.

These songs also express the range of emotion of men in process with God's mission for their lives. So often on Christian television, and some Christian books, there is talk about this level of Christian living where you're always "up" emotionally. Yet David as King wrote, *"O for the wings of a dove that I might fly away."*[1]

[1] Psalm 55:6

The Psalms show us that it's *manly* for a man to recognize his need for God, and how a man should and *can* express that need to God. That these kinds of Psalms are present in the Bible say that it's OK to express those feelings to God, even through music, and in ways with language not 'politically correct' compared to what's sung both commercially and in church today.

In his letters, Paul talked about wanting to know more of Christ. We can learn the "how" of going about it in the Psalms from men who also learned, each on his own.

Roughly half the Psalms were written by David, and at least one by Moses - men of combat, but men of sin. One beat a man to death, the other sent one of his officers to the front lines to be killed because he had had an affair with this officer's wife. And after he was caught, his song of confession was performed publicly in a service, right in front of him. Think about *that*.

So as you go through this book remember, men, *manly* men, men not afraid to fight, or to be tested, who put it all on the line be they soldiers, Spec Ops, Force Recon, SWAT, firemen, linemen, contractors, wranglers, et al, write songs to God, and God can use them in our church services.

Here's the permission slip: God *designed* men to express their emotions before Him with safety. That the Psalms were performed publicly shows the emotional security these men had both within *and* with God.

For this, Jesus is our role model, *"who, in the days of His flesh, when He had offered up prayers and supplications, with* ***vehement cries and tears*** *to Him who was able to save Him from death, and was heard because of His godly fear, though He was a Son, yet He learned obedience by the things which He suffered."* (Heb. 5:7-8, NKJV).

PRELUDE

DEFINING GOD'S ORGANIZATIONAL MODEL FOR THE NEW TESTAMENT CHURCH

To understand the role and purpose of music in the church, we must first go back to the very beginning to understand the organizational structure designed by God. God's organizational structure is elegant, simple, and flexible. It functions with as few as two. It can operate in any environment and in any time period.

With this, we must note that of all earthly organizations, the church is the *only* organization empowered by the Holy Spirit.

The church is *purposed* by God. As an organization, the church is to proclaim the Good News, train, and launch individuals into the work of service God set in place for each individual before the foundations of the earth were laid. In our culture, wherever that might be, we're to be salt and light.

Examining Christ's mission statement in Luke 4:18-19, we see that the church, empowered by the Holy Spirit, is sent to those who are broken, blind, imprisoned, crushed by life, and financially destitute, with the message, *"Change your mind about what you're thinking and doing for the Kingdom of God is at hand."* For those who commit to following Christ, the church's mission is to help rebuild those broken individuals, sending them out to be salt and light (see Eph. 4:12).

Those who commit to following Christ[1] are called by the same term in Greek as were the Israelites Moses lead out of Egypt – *the called out ones (from a larger group)*, which in Greek is *ekklesia* (the principle term for *church* used throughout this book). To use *ekklesia* is to support in daily action the definition of salvation, which is to be saved *from* something *to* something.

The first use of *ekklesia* in the New Testament is found in Matthew 16:18 where Jesus says to Peter, *"upon this rock I shall build my ekklesia and the gates of hell shall not prevail against it."*

---

[1] My wording follows the thinking of A.W. Tozer who pointed out that Christ called us to *follow* Him, not *accept* him, which is the more current evangelical phrase. To Peter, Andrew, James and John, Jesus said, *"Come now and I will build you into fishers of men"* (Mark 1:17). As we'll learn, music is one of the tools God uses to build men. And women.

Another translation for *ekklesia* is the *assembly*. In Greek culture, it meant a ruling government assembly. In his book, *Rediscovering God's Church*, Derek Prince points out that in Greek culture, slaves, women, and others were excluded from being part of the local assembly (*ekklesia*). There was, and is, no such exclusion in God's assembly.

In the *ekklesia*, every one belongs and has a place. That place is determined by their spiritual gift, which is a special gracing by the Holy Spirit to empower individuals within the *ekklesia* to go out to proclaim, to teach, to shepherd, to build one another up, to encourage, and so on. God calls this aspect of the *ekklesia* being the body of Christ. We are *the called out ones*, and *the called out ones* function as a single moving team, like the physical body of Christ, where everyone belongs and has a role and a purpose.

To paraphrase from geometry, with the *ekklesia*, the whole is *greater* than the sum of its parts.

Within the *ekklesia* are a group of leaders selected by the people who administrate and lead the organization. Here, the New Testament *ekklesia* follows a pattern that Moses' father-in-law, Jethro, gave him for the Israelite *ekklesia*. These positions are not defined by spiritual gifts. These positions are those of the elders, and literally, from the Greek, the table waiters (*diakonias*, or *deacons*).

Into God's organizational model of the church, the *ekklesia*, He adds music, which plays an important role by edifying through nurturing, challenging, consoling, and encouraging individually and collectively through effective lyrics and performances.

If the word used by Jesus, *ekklesia*, means *assembly*, then what does the word *church* mean? According to the American Heritage Dictionary, *church* is from the Middle English *chirche* which comes from the old English *cirice* which comes from Middle Greek and means *house of the Lord*. So we have a conflict where Scripture says one thing and the translators something else. Linguistically, *ekklesia* or *assembly* refers to the people, while the word *church* refers to the *building*.

You don't edify a building, you edify the people. The gates of hell do not prevail against the *ekklesia*, the people. So, when the assembly gathers there is to be edification and interaction. Into this, God brings music to edify *the called out ones*.

CHAPTER 1

THE FIRST FORMAL PURPOSING OF SONG

The first time we see music purposed in a formal way is in I Chronicles 25:1-7. Reading below, in the NIV translation, you'll see three purposes each of which becomes its own type of song. I discovered that this is a very common practice in the Bible where a word describing an action becomes a type of song. This purposing, as defined by God through David is continued by Paul in the New Testament church, but with less structure. In this chapter, I'm defining the purposes, but in Chapter 2, I'm devoting special emphasis on the prophetic song because of Paul's emphasis on the importance of prophecy and its purpose in the New Testament church.

Here's the passage:

1 David, together with the commanders of the army, set apart some of the sons of Asaph, Heman and Jeduthun for the ministry of prophesying, accompanied by harps, lyres and cymbals.

Here is the list of the men who performed this service:

2 From the sons of Asaph: Zaccur, Joseph, Nethaniah and Asarelah. The sons of Asaph were under the supervision of Asaph, who ***prophesied*** *under the king's supervision.*

3 As for Jeduthun, from his sons: Gedaliah, Zeri, Jeshaiah, Shimei, Hashabiah and Mattithiah, six in all, under the supervision of their father Jeduthun, who ***prophesied****, using the harp in* ***thanking*** *and* ***praising*** *the Lord.*

4 As for Heman, from his sons: Bukkiah, Mattaniah, Uzziel, Shubael and Jerimoth; Hananiah, Hanani, Eliathah, Giddalti and Romamti-Ezer; Joshbekashah, Mallothi, Hothir and Mahazioth.

5 All these were sons of Heman the king's seer. They were given him through the promises of God to exalt him. God gave Heman fourteen sons and three daughters.

[6]*All these men were under the supervision of their fathers for the music of the temple of the Lord, with cymbals, lyres and harps, for the ministry at the house of God.*

Asaph, Jeduthun and Heman were under the supervision of the king. [7]*Along with their relatives--all of them trained and skilled in music for the Lord--they numbered 288.*

So the three purposes are:

1. To be ***prophetic*** and to build the *ekklesia*
2. To offer ***testimony*** (thanks) about the historic acts of God in a person's life
3. To ***praise*** God

DEFINING OUR TERMS

In quality control training, you learn to define terms so that everyone knows what you're talking about by using the same definition. Similarly, because we want a Scriptural foundation for writing Christian music, we'll neither guess, assume, nor take an opinion poll as to what these words mean. Instead, I'm defining them using the same resources as professional Bible translators.

The three words in the order of use I'm defining are *prophecy*, *thanks* and *praise*. Each word, musically, also represents a specific *type* of Biblical song. The first is *prophetic*. The second, a song of *testimony*, and the third, a *shout* to the Lord. The purpose of all three, as further defined by Paul, is to edify (build up) the *ekklesia* (church).

As we'll see in Chapters 5 and 6, the Bible has specific examples of each type that we'll study for lyric content.

PROPHECY

The Hebrew word for prophecy is *naba*. In Greek, *propheteuo* is used both in the Septuagint and New Testament. Both words mean *to speak or sing under inspiration*. (**Note:** Depending on your denominational affiliation, the word *prophecy* can be a *hot* word. Some may prefer the word *proclaim*. But, by understanding what the word means, the concept should be acceptable across denominational lines.)

The purpose of a prophetic song is to warn, and to encourage, to build up the body. Charles Hodge, author of *Hodge's Theology*, in his commentary on I Corinthians 14 noted that, *"the prophet spoke with a view to **strengthening**... He strengthened the church either by **encouragement** by **comfort**, either by arousing believers to do or suffer or by pouring into their hearts the consolations of the Spirit."*

So that's what a prophetic song does. The lyrics encourage. They comfort. The end result, to use an overworked phrase from the '70s, is to encourage believers *to keep on keeping on* with an eye to finishing the race set before them

Because of the importance that Paul assigned to prophecy in the New Testament church, Chapter 2 deals specifically with the lyric content and impact of a prophetic song.

THANKS

The word for thanksgiving in Hebrew is *yadah* which literally means *to use the hand*. It's a picture of hands either being wrung or lifted up, reaching out. Its purpose is to say, *"God saves, God delivers, God rescues."* Isn't this what both the churched and the unchurched need to hear? The Bible only has one example of a *yadah*, and we'll examine it in Chapter 5 to see how it was constructed. Looking back to I Chronicles, there's to be prophetic impact that builds the Body through songs of thanksgiving or testimony, the picture of which is arms reaching out to God.

PRAISE

The three Hebrew words translated *praise*, are *barak*, *tehilla*, and *halal*. We'll see these types of songs in Chapters 3, 4 and 5.

But in the passage from I Chronicles 25:1-3, the word translated *praise* is more properly translated *shout*, or, *a soldier's victory shout*. When that Hebrew word is traced through the Scriptures, we discover that we are to make *a soldier's victory shout* to the Lord, and men are to make *a soldier's victory shout* about their *wives* in the gates of the city. So the same word that tells me to "shout" to the Lord in victory, also tells me that I'm to shout victoriously *about* my wife in the gates of the city.

The very first use of *halal* is in Genesis. After seeing the beauty of Sarah, the princes run back to Pharaoh and shout about her. Another translation could be *rave*. They *raved* about Sarah and her beauty. We *rave* about our wives in public. We *rave* about the Lord to others and to Him. If we but apply this simple idea, we discover that individual groups, nations, and regions have their own idea of what a victory shout is. For example:

US Army – *Hoo-ahhh!*
US Navy Seals – *Hoo-YAH!*
Marine Corp – *Oo-rah!*
Old South – *Rebel yell*

There's no "politically correct" Biblical term the Bible says to use when shouting to the Lord or shouting about (not at!) our wives. Whatever is a shout of victory in our language or culture is the one God expects us to use verbally and in song when we sing to him.

Going back to the text, there's to be prophetic impact through songs that shout to the Lord.

Denominational note. For some denominations and churches, shouting to the Lord might be considered out of place, inappropriate and disrespectful. If your denomination holds this view, then you'll have to evaluate that in light of what this chapter covers.

CHAPTER 2

THE PROPHETIC SONG

In this chapter we'll consider the prophetic song. The first prophetic song is the one God dictated to Moses to be taught to each Israelite. Next, we'll look at the purpose of prophecy in the New Testament church. We'll spend the most time looking at prophecy in the *ekklesia* because of its power to speak to the hearts of both the churched and unchurched.

THE VERY FIRST PROPHETIC SONG

The very first prophetic song was dictated by God to Moses. It's found in Deuteronomy 32:1-43, called *The Song of Moses*. This was a specific work given to warn the Israelites about their future once they crossed the Jordan River into Canaan. God required that each Israelite learn this song and be able to sing it. We'll study the song in Chapter 4. But for now, look at the rationale God gave to Moses in Deuteronomy 31:16-21.

16 *And the LORD said unto Moses, Behold, thou shalt sleep with thy fathers; and this people will rise up, and go a whoring after the gods of the strangers of the land, whither they go to be among them, and will forsake me, and break my covenant which I have made with them.*

17 *Then my anger shall be kindled against them in that day, and I will forsake them, and I will hide my face from them, and they shall be devoured, and many evils and troubles shall befall them; so that they will say in that day, Are not these evils come upon us, because our God is not among us?*

18 *And I will surely hide my face in that day for all the evils which they shall have wrought, in that they are turned unto other gods.*

19 *Now therefore write ye this song for you, and teach it the children of Israel: put it in their mouths, that this song may be a witness for me against the children of Israel.*

20 *For when I shall have brought them into the land which I sware unto their fathers,*

that floweth with milk and honey; and they shall have eaten and filled themselves, and waxen fat; then will they turn unto other gods, and serve them, and provoke me, and break my covenant.

21 *And it shall come to pass, when many evils and troubles are befallen them, that this song shall testify against them as a witness; for it shall not be forgotten out of the mouths of their seed: for I know their imagination which they go about, even now, before I have brought them into the land which I sware.*

This song, which the Israelites were to learn, deals with the consequences of worshipping other gods, even after God has brought them out of Egypt and into the Promised Land. The thinking process of the Israelites is that, after pursuing other gods and many problems are overwhelming them, *"God is not among us."* In other words, *"It's God's fault!"*

But God gives them this song to head off that thinking, *"No! It's not that I'm not among you, it's that you drew away from me."*

Why does God give the warning? To avoid the problem! *Thus a long range purpose of a prophetic song is to warn and confront now to avoid problems later.* Read what Moses says to the Israelites in Deuteronomy 32:46-47 after teaching them the song:

"And he said unto them, Set your hearts unto all the words which I testify among you this day, which ye shall command your children to observe to do, all the words of this law. For it is not a vain thing for you; because it is your life: and through this thing ye shall prolong your days in the land, whither ye go over Jordan to possess it."

Moses' instructions are that the Israelites are to:

- Set their hearts unto all the words of the song
- Command their children to observe and to do the lyric contents
- Take seriously the warning because it's their life

The end result of this generational obedience is that they'll prolong their days in the land they're to possess. Read *Malachi* as an example of the fulfillment of God's warning which they clearly ignored.

The Song Of Moses is found in Deuteronomy 32:1-43 (see Chapter 4, pps 34-36). When you read through it, ask yourself these questions:

1. Would you be permitted to sing this song, or any prophetic song that speaks with such directness, in your church?
2. If it was sung, what would happen? Would anyone get fired? Would anyone leave the church?
3. After reading *The Song of Moses*, what does it tell you about God's purpose in using music within the *ekklesia*?

When you read the song, you have to come away understanding that God gave this song in love so that the *ekklesia* (the Greek term for the Israelites in the Septuagint) would be blessed and successful in the plan God had for their lives for generations to come in the specific geographic area God assigned them to.

PROPHETIC SONG & PAUL

In the New Testament, we have no example of a prophetic song. What we have is Paul's instruction, that we're applying to creating new songs as David did for the Levitical music staff serving initially at the Tent of Meeting.

Paul teaches that to have a prophetic impact, the lyrics must *edify*, *exhort* and *console*.

"But he that prophesieth speaketh unto men to edification, and exhortation, and comfort." (I Corinthians 14:3)

DEFINING OUR TERMS

So that there's no question about what Paul is instructing, we go to Greek grammar resources for our definitions.

Edification - is from a Greek construction term, *oikodome*, which means to build or to build up a structure.

Exhortation - is from *paraklesis* which means to summon for help, to call near, to request or plea, to encourage, to caution, to warn, to console and comfort, to use words to stir up positive thoughts and actions.

Comfort - is *paramuthia* which means any talk whether made for the purpose of persuading, or of arousing and stimulating, or of calming and consoling.

So, a prophetic song that edifies helps to build believers from the ground up, or in some cases, builds on a foundation already in place in their lives. Prophetic songs that exhort, like the *Song of Moses*, warn, but they also caution, console and comfort, and stir people up by encouraging positive thoughts and actions. Prophetic songs persuade believers to do the right thing.

What you have to come away with is that words spoken to believers are important and have purpose. When written in song, they stay in people's minds for years. I see this as a mandate to develop the writer's craft so that we're clear that what we're putting into people's minds and souls through our music is Biblical.

PROPHETIC SONG & THOSE TO WHOM CHRIST WAS SENT

Since prophetic songs edify, exhort and comfort, it stands to reason they can also impact the people to whom we proclaim the good news. Who doesn't need encouragement? Who doesn't need to be warned at times? Who doesn't need consolation? Compare the definitions of these three words to Christ's mission statement in Luke 4:18. I've broken the passage into a list to better see those to whom He was sent.

"The Spirit of the Lord is upon me,
because he hath anointed me
to preach the gospel to the poor;
he hath sent me to heal the brokenhearted
to preach deliverance to the captives
and recovering of sight to the blind
to set at liberty them that are bruised..."

Here are the key words and definitions from Jesus' Mission Statement in chart form.

Greek Word	KJV Translation	Definition (Thayer & Smith)
Ptochos	*Poor*	Beggars, total impoverishment
Laomai	*Heal*	To heal, make whole
Suntribo	*Brokenhearted*	To break, to break in pieces, to tread down, to break down, to crush, to tear one's body and to shatter one's strength

Aphesis	*Deliverance*	Release from bondage or imprisonment
Aichmalotos	*Captive*	Captive
Thrauo	*Bruised*	Also means broken in pieces

Pause and think about this. We proclaim to those who are decidedly poor, the emotionally broken, those who are held captive or are in some type of bondage, and the physically blind and other maladies considered impossible to heal, leaving people feeling hopeless.

So, Christian song lyrics that warn, exhort and encourage, help to build up and to rebuild those who've been crushed by life's events, both followers and non-followers of Christ.

But from whom do such prophetic songs come?

They come from those of us who are called and empowered to create God's music who also, once, were broken and needed rebuilding. When speaking of the *"long night"* in II Corinthians 1:4 where they despaired of life, Paul wrote that they went through these experiences to prepare those coming behind them.

Thus, it's fair to say that we write prophetic songs:

1. To prepare those coming behind us
2. To console and encourage those living through difficult times
3. To draw non-believers to God because they identify with our experiences and how we express them.

> *Writing such songs requires vulnerability. As creators, we first learn to be vulnerable by singing, playing and writing to God. Next, we learn how to be vulnerable in song by studying those Biblical events which inspired Biblical songs, and seeing how songwriters like David, Asaph, Heman and others did it.*

Music that operates in this manner heralds (*kerusso*) the good news (*euaggelion*) because the song or composition is a testimony of what God has done and is continually doing in our lives *right now*. To do that, is to be "real" with people through song, something our Western culture desperately needs at this hour. In short, our willingness to be open through song can bring hope to others.

CHAPTER 3

HOW GOD USES MUSIC TO EDIFY

In I Corinthians 14, we learned that prophecy's role within the gathering is to edify or build up the *ekklesia*. The question is, *"How does music do this?"*[1] To understand the answer, we need to study God's instruction to Joshua for success.

GOD'S COMMAND TO JOSHUA

"Only you be strong and very courageous, that you may do according to all the law which Moses, My servant commanded you. Turn not from it to the right hand or to the left, that you may prosper wherever you go. This Book of the Law shall not depart out of your mouth, but you shall meditate on it day and night, that you may observe and do according to all that is written in it. For then you shall make your way prosperous, and then you shall deal wisely and have good success." (Joshua 1:7-8, Amplified Bible)

DEFINING OUR TERMS

For our purposes, the two key words in this passage are *depart* and *meditate*.

Depart - in Hebrew is *mush*. In English, *depart* from a Hebrew perspective is almost like a double negative. It's saying, "don't not let this happen, instead, *do*..."

Meditate - in Hebrew is *hagah*. Hagah means to *murmur* (in pleasure or anger); to whisper, speak or talk softly. By implication to *ponder*: - imagine, meditate, mourn, mutter, roar, speak, study, talk, utter. With *hagah*, you can murmur quietly to others or to yourself.[2]

So, God is telling Joshua to softly, or in a whisper, talk to himself repeating Scripture.

---

[1] Ad agencies and secular music understand these concepts but use them from a much different perspective.

[2] Marcus Aurelius observed that to know what someone really thinks, listen to what they say under their breath.

In Ephesians 5:19, Paul repeats this instruction when he says, *"speaking to yourselves."* What we are to speak/sing to ourselves is Scripture, psalms, hymns, and spiritual odes. Singing Scripture to ourselves and others is clear. But the other three song types are from ancient Greece. We'll consider them later.

Important! Paul's teaching about the use of music in the *ekklesia* comes directly from Deuteronomy 31 and 32, and Joshua 1. What you'll learn in this chapter is how God designed man to use words and music to shape the soul so that we might be successful in finishing the race God has set before each of us to run.[3]

HAGAH & BIBLICAL MURMURING

Not all translations translate *hagah* as murmuring.

Hagah	**to murmur**
NIV	*meditate*
NKJV	*meditate*
Holman	*recite it day and night*
NLT	*meditate*
RSV	*meditate*
Good News	*read in your worship. Study it day and night.*
New Century	*study it day and night*

Of all these popular translations, only Holman translates it fully. To verify this, see Job 27:4, Psalms 35:28, 37:30, 71:24, 115:7.

In Psalms 28:12 and 77:12, *hagah* is used twice; one time translated *talk* (or speak) and the other time, *meditate.*

To *hagah* is really a double action of talking to myself and pondering what I'm saying or *singing* softly to myself.[4]

[3] Depending on the kind of music listened to and sung under our breath, music lyrics can have the reverse effect.

[4] There is a large body of work in the secular arena that many technically refer to as *self-talk*. Looking at various translations, starting with the King James, and how they've translated *hagah*, you can see that many are uncomfortable with instructing someone to talk or sing Scripture to themselves. Yet, how many people learn to play basic piano and guitar so they can do just that?

Practical Applications Of Hagah

We mutter under our breath (talking to ourselves) and we sing to ourselves. Summarizing the use of *hagah* in the Psalms, we sing:

- Scripture set to music
- Wisdom set to music
- Focusing on the nature of God
- The works and the doings of God around us, in our lives, in other's lives
- The historic acts of God from the Creation,[5] to His acting in our lives and the lives of others

But why? What is God's purposing? What happens when we do this?

Practical End Results For The Individual

The Angel of the Lord in Joshua 1:7-8 tells Joshua that the end result of murmuring Scripture to ourselves is that within the mission God has called us to,

1. Our way will be made prosperous
2. We'll know how to deal wisely
3. We'll have good success

God wants us to succeed at what He's called us to do.

Thus, part of the mission of the Christian songwriter and composer is to help facilitate and encourage others to finish running the race and complete the work each of us has been called to walk in by creating works worth murmuring softly to ourselves and pondering.[6]

[5] As an example, Solomon wrote in the Psalms, *"Go to the ant, thou sluggard, and learn its ways."*

[6] Ephesians 2:10

THE INTERNAL PROCESS OF EDIFICATION

Proverbs 23:7 explains how God brings this about.

As a man thinks in his heart, so is he.

DEFINING OUR TERMS

Thinks - the word translated *thinks* in this passage is the Hebrew word *sha'ar*, which means *to act as a gatekeeper.*[7]

Heart - in Hebrew is *nephesh,* which is most often translated, *soul,* or *soul of life.* Its first use is in Genesis where at creation every living creature, including man, was given a *nephesh*. What man was given that the other living creatures weren't given was the *neshamah,* the very breath of God, blown into man. [8]

Thus the relationship:

Gatekeeper ⇨ *Soul*

The picture painted by Solomon is:

That to which a man opens the gate to his mind, is what he becomes in his nephesh (soul, heart, life).

Important! Christian lyric writing and songwriting is serious business because of the long range impact memorizing a song's lyrics and singing them to one's self can have. The emotional range of expression we find in the Psalms is very wide, but within limits. As songwriters and lyricists, we must go to the Psalms to see what those boundaries are.

EVALUATING LYRIC CONTENT

Since the core performance issue is deciding if a song's lyric should be used, knowing it will pass from the mind to the heart, how, then, do we evaluate lyrics? From Scripture, I've created five subjective tests.

[7] This is *sha'ar's* only use in the Old Testament.

[8] For a detailed reading about the *nephesh*, please see E.W. Bullinger's *The Companion Bible, Appendix 13: The Use of Nephesh in the Old Testament*. Dr. Bullinger counts the use of *nephesh* over 754 times where it's translated as *soul* 472 times. The remaining 282 uses are translated 44 different ways.

Test 1: Scripture

God wants us to sing Scripture.

Test 2: The Agape Love Test

In my book *Love Tools*, I put forth this definition of God's love (*agapao* from the Greek):

God's love is a love that chooses, regardless of how you feel, to respect, honor, show care/concern, appreciation and affection for another; regardless of whether you or the other person has earned it or deserves it.

Whether evaluating a lyric or movie or a TV show, the question to be asked is, "How does the total content or overall effect demonstrate or teach respect, honor, care/concern, appreciation, affection, repentance, or forgiveness?"

Test 3: The Good Test

The Good test is where we evaluate by God's own definition of good, as in, *"It was good."* Good in Hebrew means:

"that which is good to the senses, agreeable, pleasant and desirable; beautiful, fair; useful, fit and suitable; of that which is morally good, honest, becoming and virtuous; of that which is right. It's also applied to things prosperous and abundant; to happiness and joyfulness; to advantage and pleasure." (New Wilson's Old Testament Word Studies)

By God's definition, is the purpose and total content *good*?

Test 4: The Noble Test

The Noble Test is from Paul's command found in Philippians 4:8 (NIV):

"Finally, brothers, whatever is true, whatever is noble, whatever is right, whatever is pure, whatever is lovely, whatever is admirable - if anything is excellent or praiseworthy - think about such things."

Is it admirable? Is it true? Is it noble? Is it right? Is it pure? Is it lovely? Is it excellent? Is it praiseworthy? The point is this. If it's OK to think about it, it's OK to sing it!

TEST 5: THE MOCKER TEST

The Mocker Test is found in Psalm 1:1 (NIV):

"Blessed is the man who does not walk in the counsel of the wicked or stand in the way of sinners or sit in the seat of mockers."

What type of counsel does the lyric content give? Does it mock?[9]

CONCLUSION

Christian lyrics build.

[9] By mocking or bad counsel, I'm not referring to songs in works like musicals or operas where the purpose of such a song is to establish the nature, attitude and thinking of a character. For example, in *Camelot*, Mordred, King Arthur's son, sings *The 7 Deadly Virtues*, a song that mocks everything his father stands for. In Isaiah, God talks to Satan in a mocking tone when he calls him the morning star. So you have to check for the dramatic context of the presentation.

CHAPTER 4

22 TYPES OF BIBLICAL SONGS BY CONTENT

What *kinds* of lyrics build? And what *subjects* can a Christian song be about beyond praise and worship? This chapter begins answering these two questions by giving you most of the *shi'yrs* (songs) in the Old Testament presented in the order in which they appear in Scripture. For each song, except for *Song of Solomon* because of the length, I've given you the complete song lyric in the King James version, the subject of the song, and starting songwriting principles. So for convenience, I've put all the *shi'yrs* into this chapter, making it a quick reference tool.

Many of these songs are about events rooted in Biblical history. To fully understand what's going on, read the history in the Bible, then with a Bible atlas locate the events geographically. Even so, as you read through these song lyrics, as a writer, you need to observe that through the inspiration of the Holy Spirit, they were written so that anyone, churched or unchurched, could hear and understand with little theological instruction.

At the time they were written, all of these songs had a melody, harmony and musical accompaniment. At first glance, it's clear they're not in the song forms we know and sing in our culture. So, our primary focus is on lyric content to guide us in writing our own songs.

I've kept to the King James because it's in the public domain. My only change has been to break the lines into shorter, more songlike phrases. You're encouraged to read the same lyric in different translations.

If it's your intent to set Scripture to music, then you must know that only the King James Version is in the public domain. Thus, to create a copyright of your work, you'll need to do a partial translation or paraphrase of the passage.

LANGUAGE RESOURCES FOR SONGWRITERS

To aid you, in both study and lyric writing, I suggest you get eSword at www.e-sword.net. eSword is the complete Old and New Testaments in KJV with Strong's numbering over each word. You also get at no charge, Greek and Hebrew dictionaries so that as a word is highlighted, its definition appears.

You would also do well to download the Septuagint (and order the printed version) which also has the Strong's numbering above each Greek word with the translation below it. You can find this at http://septuagint-interlinear-greek-bible.com.

At Bible.org you can download the new New English Translation for the Old and New Testaments with over 60,000 translators notes.

HOW TO USE THIS CHAPTER

1. Read through each song type
2. Carefully take note of the content of each song and the tone behind it
3. Read the lyric aloud and listen to the rhythm of the words both in the King James and other translations
4. Compare translations
5. Look for coloristic words and phrases

APPLICATION

As an exercise, you might try creating a new song in a musical style you're comfortable in for each kind of song presented in this chapter.

Song 1: A Saga Song Of God

The first song appears in Exodus 15:1-19. We could title this song *The Horse and The Rider* for here in song, Moses relates the story of God's deliverance of the Hebrews after crossing the Red Sea. The lyric also illustrates that, *"Vengeance is mine; I will repay, saith the Lord."* (Rom. 12:19), and how the Lord protects us from enemies when we pray and ask. It's similar to a saga, but it could be considered a longer praise song.

1 I will sing unto the Lord,
for he hath triumphed gloriously:
the horse and his rider
hath he thrown into the sea.
2 The Lord is my strength and song,
and he is become my salvation:
he is my God,
and I will prepare him an habitation;
my father's God, and I will exalt him.
3 The Lord is a man of war:
the Lord is his name.

4 Pharaoh's chariots and his host
hath he cast into the sea:
his chosen captains also are drowned
in the Red sea.
5 The depths have covered them:
they sank into the bottom as a stone.

6 Thy right hand, O Lord,
is become glorious in power:
thy right hand, O Lord,
hath dashed in pieces the enemy.
7 And in the greatness of thine excellency
thou hast overthrown them
that rose up against thee:
thou sentest forth thy wrath,
which consumed them as stubble.

8 And with the blast of thy nostrils
the waters were gathered together,
the floods stood upright as an heap,
and the depths were congealed
in the heart of the sea.
9 The enemy said,
I will pursue, I will overtake,
I will divide the spoil;
my lust shall be satisfied upon them;
I will draw my sword,
my hand shall destroy them.

10 Thou didst blow with thy wind,
the sea covered them:
they sank as lead in the mighty waters.
11 Who is like unto thee, O Lord, among the gods?
who is like thee,
glorious in holiness,
fearful in praises,
doing wonders?
12 Thou stretchedst out thy right hand,
the earth swallowed them.

13 Thou in thy mercy
hast led forth the people
which thou hast redeemed:
thou hast guided them in thy strength
unto thy holy habitation.
14 The people shall hear, and be afraid:
sorrow shall take hold on the inhabitants of Palestina.
15 Then the dukes of Edom shall be amazed;
the mighty men of Moab,
trembling shall take hold upon them;
all the inhabitants of Canaan shall melt away.
16 Fear and dread shall fall upon them;
by the greatness of thine arm
they shall be as still as a stone;
till thy people pass over,
O Lord, till the people pass over,
which thou hast purchased.

17 *Thou shalt bring them in,*
and plant them in
the mountain of thine inheritance,
in the place, O Lord,
which thou hast made
for thee to dwell in,
in the Sanctuary, O Lord,
which thy hands have established.

18 *The Lord shall reign for ever and ever.*
19 *For the horse of Pharaoh*
went in with his chariots
and with his horsemen into the sea,
and the Lord brought again
the waters of the sea upon them;
but the children of Israel
went on dry land in the midst of the sea.

PRINCIPLE 1:

What makes a Godly song is a lyric celebrating an act of God's deliverance for either an individual or a nation.

The lyric both praises God and cites the historical action, recording God's deliverance with beautiful and vivid imagery. Here's an important point. What separates *The Horse and The Rider* from an epic like *The Song of Beowulf* or *El Cid* is that *The Horse and The Rider* glorifies an historical act of God in a nation's life, while *The Song of Beowulf*, glorifies the exploits and adventures of a single individual. One's focus is the historic action of God in the believer's life teaching the pragmatic value of dependence on God, the other's focus is on individual exploits. The difference is that our sagas reflect a culture with Yahweh at its center who guides the hero through a predetermined mission. There is nothing left to chance. Fate has nothing to do with it.

PRINCIPLE 2:

Our hero is God and we sing of His exploits alone and in our lives.

Biblical sagas do not have heroes running off pursuing their own adventures with reckless abandon as has been written about by Joseph Campbell in *The Power of Myth* and *The Hero With a Thousand Faces*. With God, no one goes off on an adventure just for the sake of the adventure. Our God is a mission directed God. Going off on an adventure of our choosing without God's full blessing and timing always leads to disaster for the believer.

For example, Moses, after beating the Egyptian to death (in anger at his beating of a Hebrew slave) assumed that the Israelites understood that he had come to Goshen to side with them and liberate them (see Acts 7:25). It's important to note that Moses came to this decision and subsequent action all alone. No where in the Exodus text do we see that God instructed Moses to go down to Goshen to begin the liberation process. While we know that it was God's will for Moses to liberate the Hebrews, the choice of timing at that point, was Moses', not God's. So when Moses saw that the Israelites didn't grasp that his beating of an Egyptian to death was a signal of liberation, he fled Egypt.

To underscore this principle, God directs Moses, as the writer of the Torah, to tell this aspect of God's story through him so that all who read the Torah would understand the danger of pursuing the mission without God's blessing or timing. What God wants from us is the *attitude* of an adventurer operating under the *direction* of His chosen mission and timing for our lives.

Principle 3:

When dealing with individuals or nations, the song can model the bold attitude of the adventurer who's clearly operating under God's orders.

We make a mistake if we think that God's music is to be confined to the Temple or the church. Consider this interesting passage from *Deborah's Song* (Judges 5:11, NLT):

Listen to the village musicians gathered at the watering holes
They recount the righteous victories of the Lord
and the victories of his villagers in Israel
Then the people of the Lord
marched down to the city gates.

Here we see two types of song lyrics performed by the village musicians or singers:

1. The righteous victories of the Lord
2. The victories, or righteous acts, of his warriors in Israel

Watering holes or watering places were where people gathered in ancient times to meet each other and to get news. So now we have an acceptable social place for Israelites to be strengthened in song, and the Gentiles to become exposed to the workings of Yahweh. Note, however, that the lyric focus is on God's acts.

SONG 2: A SONG OF INSTRUCTION, WARNING & PROPHECY FROM GOD

"Now write down for yourselves this song and teach it to the Israelites and have them sing it, so that it may be a witness for me against them. When I have brought them into the land flowing with milk and honey, the land I promised on oath to their forefathers, and when they eat their fill and thrive, they will turn to other gods and worship them, rejecting me and breaking my covenant. And when many disasters and difficulties come upon them, this song will testify against them, because it will not be forgotten by their descendants. I know what they are disposed to do, even before I bring them into the land I promised them on oath." So Moses wrote down this song that day and taught it to the Israelites. (Deuteronomy 31:19-22, NIV)

The second song in Scripture, written by God (called by scholars *The Song of Moses*) is a prophetic warning. Its function is to instruct, encourage, warn and prophesy for generations so that believers understand that the issues in their lives are the result of their choosing disobedience and not the result of God's abandonment. God's purpose for this song is very clear: to be a testimony against the Israelites because God knows what they are disposed to do. Moses was instructed to teach every Israelite this song before Joshua took over from him. Here it is in the KJV from Deuteronomy 32:1-43.

1 Give ear, O ye heavens, and I will speak;
and hear, O earth, the words of my mouth.

2 My doctrine shall drop as the rain,
my speech shall distil as the dew,
as the small rain upon the tender herb,
and as the showers upon the grass:
3 Because I will publish the name of the Lord:
ascribe ye greatness unto our God.

4 He is the Rock,
his work is perfect:
for all his ways are judgment:
a God of truth and without iniquity,
just and right is he.

5 They have corrupted themselves,
their spot is not the spot of his children:
they are a perverse and crooked generation.
6 Do ye thus requite the Lord,
O foolish people and unwise?
is not he thy father that hath bought thee?
hath he not made thee, and established thee?

7 Remember the days of old,
consider the years of many generations:
ask thy father, and he will shew thee;
thy elders, and they will tell thee.
8 When the most High divided to the nations their inheritance,
when he separated the sons of Adam,
he set the bounds of the people
according to the number of the children of Israel.

9 For the Lord's portion is his people;
Jacob is the lot of his inheritance.
10 He found him in a desert land,
and in the waste howling wilderness;
he led him about, he instructed him,
he kept him as the apple of his eye.
11 As an eagle stirreth up her nest,

fluttereth over her young,
spreadeth abroad her wings,
taketh them, beareth them on her wings:

12 *So the Lord alone did lead him,*
and there was no strange god with him.
13 *He made him ride on the high places of the earth,*
that he might eat the increase of the fields;
and he made him to suck honey out of the rock,
and oil out of the flinty rock;
14 *Butter of kine,*
and milk of sheep,
with fat of lambs,
and rams of the breed of Bashan,
and goats, with the fat of kidneys of wheat;
and thou didst drink the pure blood of the grape.

15 *But Jeshurun waxed fat,*
and kicked:
thou art waxen fat,
thou art grown thick,
thou art covered with fatness;
then he forsook God which made him,
and lightly esteemed the Rock of his salvation.
16 *They provoked him to jealousy with strange gods,*
with abominations provoked they him to anger.

17 *They sacrificed unto devils,*
not to God;
to gods whom they knew not,
to new gods that came newly up,
whom your fathers feared not.

18 *Of the Rock that begat thee thou art unmindful,*
and hast forgotten God that formed thee.
19 *And when the Lord saw it,*
he abhorred them,
because of the provoking of his sons,
and of his daughters.

20 *And he said,*
I will hide my face from them,
I will see what their end shall be:
for they are a very froward generation,
children in whom is no faith.

21 *They have moved me to jealousy with that which is not God;*
they have provoked me to anger with their vanities:
and I will move them to jealousy with those which are not a people;
I will provoke them to anger with a foolish nation.

22 *For a fire is kindled in mine anger,*
and shall burn unto the lowest hell,
and shall consume the earth with her increase,
and set on fire the foundations of the mountains.
23 *I will heap mischiefs upon them;*
I will spend mine arrows upon them.
24 *They shall be burnt with hunger,*
and devoured with burning heat,
and with bitter destruction:
I will also send the teeth of beasts upon them,
with the poison of serpents of the dust.
25 *The sword without,*
and terror within,
shall destroy both the young man and the virgin,
the suckling also with the man of gray hairs.

26 *I said, I would scatter them into corners,*
I would make the remembrance of them
to cease from among men:
27 *Were it not that I feared the wrath of the enemy,*
lest their adversaries should behave themselves strangely,
and lest they should say,
Our hand is high, and the Lord hath not done all this.

28 For they are a nation
void of counsel,
neither is there any understanding in them.
29 O that they were wise,
that they understood this,
that they would consider their latter end!

30 How should one chase a thousand,
and two put ten thousand to flight,
except their Rock had sold them,
and the Lord had shut them up?
31 For their rock is not as our Rock,
even our enemies themselves being judges.

32 For their vine is of the vine of Sodom,
and of the fields of Gomorrah:
their grapes are grapes of gall,
their clusters are bitter:

33 Their wine is the poison of dragons,
and the cruel venom of asps.
34 Is not this laid up in store with me,
and sealed up among my treasures?
35 To me belongeth vengeance,
and recompence;
their foot shall slide in due time:
for the day of their calamity is at hand,
and the things that shall come upon them
make haste.

36 For the Lord shall judge his people,
and repent himself for his servants,
when he seeth that their power is gone,
and there is none shut up, or left.
37 And he shall say,
Where are their gods,
their rock in whom they trusted,
38 Which did eat the fat of their sacrifices,
and drank the wine of their drink offerings?
let them rise up and help you, and be your
protection.

39 See now that I, even I, am he, and there
is no god with me:
I kill,
and I make alive;
I wound,
and I heal:
neither is there any that can deliver out of
my hand.
40 For I lift up my hand to heaven, and say,
I live for ever.

41 If I whet my glittering sword,
and mine hand take hold on judgment;
I will render vengeance to mine enemies,
and will reward them that hate me.
42 I will make mine arrows drunk with blood,
and my sword shall devour flesh;
and that with the blood of the slain
and of the captives,
from the beginning of revenges upon the enemy.

43 Rejoice, O ye nations, with his people:
for he will avenge the blood of his servants,
and will render vengeance to his
adversaries,
and will be merciful unto his land,
and to his people.

Song 3: The Saga Song Blending God's Acts With A Specific Individual

The Song of Deborah is our example in Judges 5:2-31. God directs Deborah to list her name and sing of herself and Barak. It's never Deborah alone. This song retells the story cited in Judges 4. Compare the song to the event.

2 Praise ye the Lord
for the avenging of Israel,
when the people willingly offered themselves.
3 Hear,
O ye kings;
give ear,
O ye princes;
I, even I, will sing unto the Lord;
I will sing praise
to the Lord God of Israel.

4 Lord,
when thou wentest out of Seir,
when thou marchedst out of the field of Edom,
the earth trembled,
and the heavens dropped,
the clouds also dropped water.
5 The mountains melted
from before the Lord,
even that Sinai
from before the Lord God of Israel.

6 In the days of Shamgar the son of Anath,
in the days of Jael,
the highways were unoccupied,
and the travelers walked through byways.
7 The inhabitants of the villages ceased,
they ceased in Israel,
until that
I Deborah arose,
that I arose
a mother in Israel.
8 They chose new gods;
then was war in the gates:
was there a shield or spear
seen among forty thousand in Israel?

9 My heart is toward
the governors of Israel,
that offered themselves
willingly among the people.
Bless ye the Lord.

10 Speak,
ye that ride on white asses,
ye that sit in judgment,
and walk by the way.
11 They that are delivered
from the noise of archers
in the places of drawing water,
there shall they rehearse
the righteous acts of the Lord,
even the righteous acts
toward the inhabitants of his villages in Israel:
then shall the people of the Lord go down to the gates.

12 Awake, awake,
Deborah:
awake, awake,
utter a song:
arise, Barak,
and lead thy captivity captive,
thou son of Abinoam.
13 Then he made him that remaineth
have dominion
over the nobles among the people:
the Lord
made me have dominion over the mighty.
14 Out of Ephraim
was there a root of them against Amalek;
after thee,
Benjamin,

among thy people;
out of Machir came down governors,
and out of Zebulun
they that handle the pen of the writer.
15 And the princes of Issachar were with Deborah;
even Issachar,
and also Barak:
he was sent on foot into the valley.
For the divisions of Reuben
there were great thoughts of heart.
16 Why abodest thou among the sheepfolds,
to hear the bleatings of the flocks?
For the divisions of Reuben
there were great searchings of heart.

17 Gilead abode beyond Jordan:
and why did Dan remain in ships?
Asher continued on the sea shore,
and abode in his breaches.
18 Zebulun and Naphtali
were a people
that jeoparded their lives
unto the death
in the high places of the field.
19 The kings came and fought,
then fought the kings of Canaan in Taanach
by the waters of Megiddo;
they took no gain of money.
20 They fought from heaven;
the stars in their courses fought against Sisera.
21 The river of Kishon swept them away,
that ancient river,
the river Kishon.
O my soul,
thou hast trodden down strength.
22 Then were the horsehoofs broken
by the means of the pransings,
the pransings of their mighty ones.

23 Curse ye Meroz,
said the angel of the Lord,
curse ye bitterly the inhabitants thereof;
because they came not to the help of the Lord,
to the help of the Lord against the mighty.
24 Blessed above women
shall Jael the wife of Heber the Kenite be,
blessed shall she be
above women in the tent.
25 He asked water,
and she gave him milk;
she brought forth butter in a lordly dish.
26 She put her hand to the nail,
and her right hand to the workmen's hammer;
and with the hammer she smote Sisera,
she smote off his head,
when she had pierced and stricken through his temples.
27 At her feet he bowed,
he fell, he lay down:
at her feet he bowed,
he fell:
where he bowed,
there he fell down dead.

28 The mother of Sisera
looked out at a window,
and cried through the lattice,
Why is his chariot so long in coming?
why tarry the wheels
of his chariots?
29 Her wise ladies answered her,
yea,
she returned answer to herself,
30 Have they not sped?
have they not divided the prey;
to every man a damsel or two;
to Sisera a prey of divers colours, a prey of divers colours of needlework,
of divers colours of needlework on both sides,
meet for the necks of them that take the spoil?

31 So let all thine enemies perish,
O Lord: but let them that love him
be as the sun when he goeth forth in his might.

Principle 4:

Celebration songs recount in vivid imagery, without all the historical details, an historical action of God.

SONG 4: THE SONG OF GOD'S RESCUE OR DELIVERANCE OF AN INDIVIDUAL

This is probably the leading kind of song of all 22 types. II Samuel 22 contains a song of David's deliverance by God from his enemies and King Saul.

*1 And David spake unto the LORD the words
of this song in the day that the LORD had
delivered him out of the hand of all his
enemies, and out of the hand of Saul:*

*2 And he said, The LORD is my rock, and
my fortress, and my deliverer;
3 The God of my rock; in him will I trust:
he is my shield, and the horn of my salvation,
my high tower, and my refuge, my saviour;
thou savest me from violence.
4 I will call on the LORD, who is worthy to
be praised:
so shall I be saved from mine enemies.*

*5 When the waves of death compassed me,
the floods of ungodly men made me afraid;
6 The sorrows of hell compassed me about;
the snares of death prevented me;
7 In my distress I called upon the LORD,
and cried to my God:
and he did hear my voice out of his temple,
and my cry did enter into his ears.*

*8 Then the earth shook and trembled;
the foundations of heaven moved and shook,
because he was wroth.
9 There went up a smoke out of his nostrils,
and fire out of his mouth devoured:
coals were kindled by it.
10 He bowed the heavens also, and came down;
and darkness was under his feet.
11 And he rode upon a cherub, and did fly:
and he was seen upon the wings of the wind.
12 And he made darkness pavilions round
about him,
dark waters, and thick clouds of the skies.
13 Through the brightness before him were
coals of fire kindled.
14 The LORD thundered from heaven,
and the most High uttered his voice.
15 And he sent out arrows, and scattered them;
lightning, and discomfited them.
16 And the channels of the sea appeared,
the foundations of the world were discovered,
at the rebuking of the LORD, at the blast of
the breath of his nostrils.*

*17 He sent from above, he took me;
he drew me out of many waters;
18 He delivered me from my strong enemy,
and from them that hated me: for they were
too strong for me.
19 They prevented me in the day of my
calamity:
but the LORD was my stay.*

*20 He brought me forth also into a large
place:
he delivered me, because he delighted in me.
21 The LORD rewarded me according to my
righteousness:
according to the cleanness of my hands
hath he recompensed me.
22 For I have kept the ways of the LORD,
and have not wickedly departed from my
God.*

*23 For all his judgments were before me:
and as for his statutes, I did not depart
from them.
24 I was also upright before him, and have
kept myself from mine iniquity.
25 Therefore the LORD hath recompensed*

me according to my righteousness;
according to my cleanness in his eye sight.

26 With the merciful thou wilt shew thyself merciful,
and with the upright man thou wilt shew thyself upright.
27 With the pure thou wilt shew thyself pure;
and with the froward thou wilt shew thyself unsavoury.
28 And the afflicted people thou wilt save:
but thine eyes are upon the haughty, that thou mayest bring them down.

29 For thou art my lamp,
O LORD: and the LORD will lighten my darkness.
30 For by thee I have run through a troop:
by my God have I leaped over a wall.
31 As for God, his way is perfect;
the word of the LORD is tried: he is a buckler to all them that trust in him.
32 For who is God, save the LORD?
and who is a rock, save our God?
33 God is my strength and power:
and he maketh my way perfect.

34 He maketh my feet like hinds' feet:
and setteth me upon my high places.
35 He teacheth my hands to war;
so that a bow of steel is broken by mine arms.
36 Thou hast also given me the shield of thy salvation:
and thy gentleness hath made me great.
37 Thou hast enlarged my steps under me;
so that my feet did not slip.
38 I have pursued mine enemies, and destroyed them;
and turned not again until I had consumed them.
39 And I have consumed them, and wounded them, that they could not arise:
yea, they are fallen under my feet.
40 For thou hast girded me with strength to battle:
them that rose up against me hast thou subdued under me.
41 Thou hast also given me the necks of mine enemies,
that I might destroy them that hate me.
42 They looked, but there was none to save;
even unto the LORD, but he answered them not.
43 Then did I beat them as small as the dust of the earth,
I did stamp them as the mire of the street,
and did spread them abroad.

44 Thou also hast delivered me from the strivings of my people,
thou hast kept me to be head of the heathen:
a people which I knew not shall serve me.
45 Strangers shall submit themselves unto me:
as soon as they hear, they shall be obedient unto me.
46 Strangers shall fade away, and they shall be afraid out of their close places.

47 The LORD liveth; and blessed be my rock;
and exalted be the God of the rock of my salvation.
48 It is God that avengeth me, and that bringeth down the people under me,
49 And that bringeth me forth from mine enemies:
thou also hast lifted me up on high above them that rose up against me:
thou hast delivered me from the violent man.

50 Therefore I will give thanks unto thee, O LORD, among the heathen,
and I will sing praises unto thy name.
51 He is the tower of salvation for his king:
and sheweth mercy to his anointed,
unto David, and to his seed for evermore.

Consider the first verse of this song, here, using the NIV translation:

2 The Lord is my rock,
my fortress and my deliverer.
3 my God is my rock,
in whom I take refuge,
my shield,
and the horn of my salvation.
He is my stronghold,
my refuge and my savior
from violent men you save me.
4 I call to the Lord,
who is worthy of praise,
And I am saved from my enemies.

The first verse of this song cites the end result, the action that God has done.

The second verse, describes the situation emotionally, not historically. Not only does David express what he's feeling, but he does so by giving vivid word pictures describing what he's feeling.

5 The waves of death swirled around me;
the torrents of destruction overwhelmed me.
6 The cords of the grave coiled around me,
the snares of death confronted me

PRINCIPLE 5:

The rescue situation can be described emotionally with vivid word pictures, and not just historically.

PRINCIPLE 6:

Lyrics can cite the feelings of the author and are best done so through vivid word pictures with lots of imagery so that others understand what the writer is feeling.

Principle 7:

We can use simile's to describe God and to describe what His actions are like, in this Psalm, like a fire-breathing dragon.

The third verse describes God's response, much like an old time western where the US Cavalry gets the word from a runner that a wagon train is in trouble and begins to mount up for the rescue.

8 The earth trembled and quaked
the foundations of the heavens shook
they trembled because he was angry.
9 Smoke rose from his nostrils
consuming fire came from his mouth
burning coals blazed out of it.

We know from Jesus that God is spirit. With that in mind, look at the imaginative way in which David describes God's anger over what's being done to his friend, David. The picture here portrays God's anger like a fire-breathing dragon.

Principle 8:

We can acknowledge that God rescues us because He loves us and delights in us.

The next set of verses describe the rescue in highly vivid terms. This is what the rescue felt like to David. God parts the heavens, he mounts his cherubim and flies to David's rescue, bolts of lightning blazing and routing enemies, arrows are flying. David, surrounded by his enemies and tall waves, is lifted out by God and put in a spacious space because God delights in him.

Principle 9:

We can acknowledge in music that God rescues and does things for us because we're obedient, or in our disobedience he has granted us mercy and grace.

Verses 21-25 give David's further rationale for why he was rescued, he was obedient and kept himself from sin.

Verses 26-30 praise God for the rescue and talk about God's nature.

PRINCIPLE 10:

We can acknowledge in song how effectively God has trained us for the mission.

Verses 31-37 praise God for how he's trained David and enabled him for battle, to fulfill his mission as King. Here, I think, is an often missed point. We continue to see that God is a mission directed God and that he trains us for that mission. Yet some Christians have no concept of their mission, so they can't even discuss it, much less understand, how God has trained them to speak as David has.

Verses 38-43 describe his post-rescue action. He's rested, he's ready, and now he's going back to fight and rout his enemies.

43 I beat them as fine
as the dust of the earth
I pounded
and trampled them
like mud in the streets.

PRINCIPLE 11:

We have enemies. We may sing of their defeat and our routing of them as long as we don't gloat and understand who is the Source of that victory.

In verses 44-51, we have the final results of God's victory where God is praised and we see the results in our lives of that victory.

Song 5: The Shouting Praise Song

The simplest praise song in Scripture is found in II Chronicles 5:13 (NIV):

[13]He is good,
his love endures forever.

This lyric focuses on two aspects of God in just two lines. It was sung in the temple by all the people in one voice, joined in unison by 120 priestly trumpeters and the choir, along with cymbals and other instruments.

This particular praise is called a *halal*, a shout to the Lord.

Read what happened in the temple dedication service when the people raved about God:

[11]And it came to pass, when the priests were come out of the holy place: (for all the priests
that were present were sanctified, and did not then wait by course: [12]Also the Levites which
were the singers, all of them of Asaph, of Heman, of Jeduthun, with their sons and their brethren, being arrayed in white linen, having cymbals and psalteries and harps, stood at the east end of the altar, and with them an hundred and twenty priests sounding with
trumpets:) [13]It came even to pass, as the trumpeters and singers were as one, to make one sound to be heard in praising and thanking the Lord; and when they lifted up their voice with the trumpets and cymbals and instruments of musick, and praised [halal] the Lord, saying,

For he is good;
for his mercy endureth for ever:

that then the house [indicating they stood as a family] was filled with a cloud, even the
house of the Lord; [14]So that the priests could not stand to minister [continue to contribute] by reason of the cloud: for the glory of the Lord had filled the house of God.

This verse explains Paul's statement that God inhabits the praises of his people. And we're to do it in a loud, noisy, boisterous joyous way at the start of the service.

SONG 6: MOCKING SONGS

These are not songs we're to sing, but they are songs sung by others around us who, seeing the trials and difficulties we face, mock us, as seen here in Job 30 (NIV):

9 *And now their sons mock me in song;*
I have become a byword among them.
10 *They detest me and keep their distance;*
they do not hesitate to spit in my face.
11 *Now that God has unstrung my bow*
and afflicted me,
they throw off restraint
in my presence.

Song 7: Wedding Songs

Sung by the Bride and Groom

We find a complete wedding song in Psalm 45, with this lyric created to be sung to the tune of *Lilies*. Psalm 45 is a duet for the bride and bridegroom with the promise of children to come.

Bride

1 *My heart is inditing a good matter:*
I speak of the things
which I have made
touching the king:
my tongue is the pen of a ready writer.
2 *Thou art fairer than the children of men:*
grace is poured into thy lips:
therefore God hath blessed thee for ever.
3 *Gird thy sword upon thy thigh,*
O most mighty,
with thy glory and thy majesty.
4 *And in thy majesty ride prosperously*
because of truth
and meekness
and righteousness;
and thy right hand
shall teach thee terrible things.
5 *Thine arrows are sharp*
in the heart of the king's enemies;
whereby the people fall under thee.

Groom

6 *Thy throne, O God,*
is for ever and ever:
the sceptre of thy kingdom
is a right sceptre.
7 *Thou lovest righteousness,*
and hatest wickedness:
therefore God,
thy God,
hath anointed thee
with the oil of gladness above thy fellows.
8 *All thy garments smell of myrrh,*
and aloes, and cassia,
out of the ivory palaces,
whereby they have made thee glad.
9 *Kings' daughters were among*
thy honourable women:
upon thy right hand did stand the queen
in gold of Ophir.
10 *Hearken, O daughter,*
and consider,
and incline thine ear;
forget also thine own people,
and thy father's house;
11 *So shall the king greatly desire thy beauty:*
for he is thy Lord; and worship thou him.
12 *And the daughter of Tyre*
shall be there with a gift;
even the rich among the people
shall intreat thy favour.
13 *The king's daughter*
is all glorious within:
her clothing is of wrought gold.
14 *She shall be brought unto the king*
in raiment of needlework:
the virgins
her companions that follow her
shall be brought unto thee.
15 *With gladness and rejoicing*
shall they be brought:
they shall enter into the king's palace.

Bride

16 *Instead of thy fathers shall be thy children,*
whom thou mayest make princes in all the earth.
17 *I will make thy name*
to be remembered in all generations:
therefore shall the people praise thee for ever and ever.

PRINCIPLE 12:

Songs can be sung as duets.

PRINCIPLE 13:

Wedding songs proclaim the strength and hunter/warrior aspect of the groom, and the beauty and gloriousness of the bride. The bride affirms her commitment to develop a family, and to perpetuate her husband's memory.

Song 8: The Shouting Song Of Answered Prayer

We see this in Psalm 66. When prayers are answered, we're to write a song that *halal's* the Lord, raves about him.

1 Make a joyful noise [shout] unto God,
all ye lands:
2 Sing [make music] forth the honour of his name:
make his praise [tehillah] glorious.
3 Say unto God,
How terrible art thou in thy works!
through the greatness of thy power
shall thine enemies submit themselves unto thee.
4 All the earth shall worship thee,
and shall sing unto thee;
they shall sing to thy name.

Selah.

5 Come and see the works of God:
he is terrible in his doing
toward the children of men.
6 He turned the sea into dry land:
they went through the flood on foot:
there did we rejoice in him.
7 He ruleth by his power for ever;
his eyes behold the nations:
let not the rebellious exalt themselves.

Selah.

8 O bless our God,
ye people,
and make the voice of his praise to be heard:
9 Which holdeth our soul in life,
and suffereth not our feet to be moved.
10 For thou, O God,
hast proved us:
thou hast tried us,
as silver is tried.
11 Thou broughtest us into the net;
thou laidst affliction upon our loins.
12 Thou hast caused men to ride over our heads;
we went through fire and through water:
but thou broughtest us out into a wealthy place.
13 I will go into thy house with burnt offerings:
I will pay thee my vows,
14 Which my lips have uttered,
and my mouth hath spoken,
when I was in trouble.
15 I will offer unto thee
burnt sacrifices of fatlings,
with the incense of rams;
I will offer bullocks with goats.

Selah.

16 Come and hear,
all ye that fear God,
and I will declare what he hath done for my soul.
17 I cried unto him with my mouth,
and he was extolled with my tongue.
18 If I regard iniquity in my heart,
the Lord will not hear me:
19 But verily God hath heard me;
he hath attended to the voice of my prayer.
20 Blessed be God,
which hath not turned away my prayer,
nor his mercy from me.

Principle 14:

When prayers are answered, say so in song.

SONG 9: THE HARVEST SONG

Some scholars believe that Psalm 67 is a harvest song to the Lord. If the scholars are accurate, then we need to understand that this isn't a song asking for material wealth. All farmers and fruit growers know that harvest time is a time of employment, a time for a profitable return on investment so that the farm business can continue, and a time for providing food for the population. The same concept applies for a business launching a new product. Success creates employment and economic prosperity for the local region and the nation. As I write this, California citrus growers in the Spring of 2007, had frosts that wiped out a majority of the crop. The result was substantially higher prices for citrus across the U.S., a loss of jobs locally in California, and a loss of income for the state. Thus, harvest songs sung to God are important.

1 *God be merciful unto us,*
and bless us;
and cause his face to shine upon us;

Selah.

2 *That thy way may be known upon earth,*
thy saving health among all nations.
3 *Let the people praise thee,*
O God;
let all the people praise thee.
4 *O let the nations be glad and sing for joy:*
for thou shalt judge the people righteously,
and govern the nations upon earth.

Selah.

5 *Let the people praise thee,*
O God;
let all the people praise thee.
6 *Then shall the earth yield her increase;*
and God,
even our own God,
shall bless us.
7 *God shall bless us;*
and all the ends of the earth shall fear him.

PRINCIPLE 15:

It's appropriate to write songs to God asking for business success because of the number of people positively impacted by growing businesses.

Song 10: To Punish People Who Do Evil

Here's a concept we struggle with as Christians knowing that, as Jesus said to James and John, *"For the Son of man is not come to destroy men's lives, but to save them"* (Luke 9:56). We must understand that God's punishment serves two purposes, one is to bring people low enough so that they will turn to Him. The other is to clearly deal with people who have absolutely turned from God, until such time as they choose to repent and turn back to God. It is always God's desire to bring people to Him, not damn them and chase them away.

So in Psalm 76, we have a song that deals with this issue. It speaks of the solemnity of the land and its inhabitants after God has rendered his judgment. It's a pause to think that God is indeed God.

1 In Judah is God known:
his name is great in Israel.
2 In Salem also is his tabernacle,
and his dwelling place in Zion.
3 There brake he the arrows of the bow,
the shield,
and the sword,
and the battle.

Selah.

4 Thou art more glorious and excellent
than the mountains of prey.
5 The stouthearted are spoiled,
they have slept their sleep:
and none of the men of might have
found their hands.
6 At thy rebuke,
O God of Jacob,
both the chariot and horse are cast into
a dead sleep.
7 Thou, even thou,
art to be feared:
and who may stand in thy sight when once
thou art angry?
8 Thou didst cause judgment to be heard
from heaven;
the earth feared,
and was still,
9 When God arose to judgment,
to save all the meek of the earth.

Selah.

10 Surely the wrath of man shall praise thee:
the remainder of wrath shalt thou restrain.
11 Vow, and pay unto the Lord your God:
let all that be round about him
bring presents unto him that ought to be
feared.
12 He shall cut off the spirit of princes:
he is terrible to the kings of the earth.

Principle 16:

It's appropriate to write songs to be a type of prayer or warning that motivates the listener to think twice.

SONG 11: TO FIGHT AGAINST THOSE WHO CONSPIRE AGAINST US

This song, Psalm 83 written by Asaph, is a song that reflects Asaph's understanding of the mission. Notice the directness in verse 10. This was sung in the Tent of Meeting and the Temple. Could such a lyric be sung in your church today?

1 *Keep not thou silence, O God:*
hold not thy peace,
and be not still, O God.
2 *For, lo, thine enemies make a tumult:*
and they that hate thee have lifted up the head.
3 *They have taken crafty counsel against thy people,*
and consulted against thy hidden ones.
4 *They have said,*
"Come, and let us cut them off from being a nation;
that the name of Israel may be no more in remembrance."
5 *For they have consulted together with one consent:*
they are confederate against thee:
6 *The tabernacles of Edom, and the Ishmaelites;*
of Moab, and the Hagarenes;
7 *Gebal, and Ammon,*
and Amalek;
the Philistines with the inhabitants of Tyre;
8 *Assur also is joined with them:*
they have holpen the children of Lot.

Selah.

9 *Do unto them as unto the Midianites;*
as to Sisera,
as to Jabin, at the brook of Kison:
10 *Which perished at Endor:*
they became as dung for the earth.
11 *Make their nobles like Oreb,*
and like Zeeb:
yea, all their princes as Zebah,
and as Zalmunna:
12 *Who said, "Let us take to ourselves the houses of God in possession."*

13 *O my God,*
make them like a wheel;
as the stubble before the wind.
14 *As the fire burneth a wood,*

and as the flame setteth the mountains on fire;
15 *So persecute them with thy tempest,*
and make them afraid with thy storm.
16 *Fill their faces with shame;*
that they may seek thy name, O Lord.
17 *Let them be confounded and troubled for ever;*
yea, let them be put to shame, and perish:
18 *That men may know that thou,*
whose name alone is JEHOVAH,
art the most high over all the earth.

SONG 12: THE TROUBLED SOUL

Psalm 88 was written by Heman, one of the Sons of Korah. The lyrics of this song are very direct. There are no pretty word pictures as with David. Instead, as a lyricist, Heman is emotionally direct and to the point. He can tell you what he's feeling, and he does so simply, yet eloquently. And he asks the questions that all of us look to the Lord to answer.

1 O Lord God of my salvation,
I have cried day and night before thee:
2 Let my prayer come before thee:
incline thine ear unto my cry;
3 For my soul is full of troubles:
and my life draweth nigh unto the grave.
4 I am counted with them that go down into the pit:
I am as a man that hath no strength:
5 Free among the dead,
like the slain that lie in the grave,
whom thou rememberest no more:
and they are cut off from thy hand.
6 Thou hast laid me in the lowest pit,
in darkness, in the deeps.
7 Thy wrath lieth hard upon me,
and thou hast afflicted me with all thy waves.

Selah.

8 Thou hast put away mine acquaintance far from me;
thou hast made me an abomination unto them:
I am shut up, and I cannot come forth.
9 Mine eye mourneth by reason of affliction:
Lord, I have called daily upon thee,
I have stretched out my hands unto thee.
10 Wilt thou shew wonders to the dead?
shall the dead arise and praise thee?

Selah.

11 Shall thy lovingkindness be declared in the grave?
or thy faithfulness in destruction?
12 Shall thy wonders be known in the dark?
and thy righteousness in the land of forgetfulness?
13 But unto thee have I cried,
O Lord;

and in the morning shall my prayer prevent thee.
[14]*Lord, why castest thou off my soul?*
why hidest thou thy face from me?
[15]*I am afflicted and ready to die from my youth up:*
while I suffer thy terrors I am distracted.
[16]*Thy fierce wrath goeth over me;*
thy terrors have cut me off.
[17]*They came round about me daily like water;*
they compassed me about together.
[18]*Lover and friend hast thou put far from me,*
and mine acquaintance into darkness.

Principle 17:

It's not necessary for a Christian song to always have a happy ending or God getting the glory. We can leave our questions in song out there, unanswered.

SONG 13: THE SABBATH SONG

Psalm 92, written by an anonymous lyricist, is for the Sabbath day. Note that the focus is on making merry of heart to God, and not resultant fellowship; to recall God's deeds, to be glad about them, and to sing for joy at what God does.

1 It is a good thing to give thanks unto the Lord,
and to sing praises unto thy name, O most High:
2 To shew forth thy lovingkindness in the morning,
and thy faithfulness every night,
3 Upon an instrument of ten strings,
and upon the psaltery; upon the harp with a solemn sound.
4 For thou, Lord, hast made me glad through thy work:
I will triumph in the works of thy hands.
5 O Lord, how great are thy works!
and thy thoughts are very deep.
6 A brutish man knoweth not;
neither doth a fool understand this.
7 When the wicked spring as the grass,
and when all the workers of iniquity do flourish;
it is that they shall be destroyed for ever:
8 But thou, Lord, art most high for evermore.
9 For, lo, thine enemies,
O Lord, for, lo, thine enemies shall perish;
all the workers of iniquity shall be scattered.
10 But my horn shalt thou exalt like the horn of an unicorn:
I shall be anointed with fresh oil.
11 Mine eye also shall see my desire on mine enemies,
and mine ears shall hear my desire of the wicked that rise up against me.
12 The righteous shall flourish like the palm tree:
he shall grow like a cedar in Lebanon.
13 Those that be planted in the house of the Lord
shall flourish in the courts of our God.
14 They shall still bring forth fruit in old age;
they shall be fat and flourishing;
15 To shew that the Lord is upright:
he is my rock,
and there is no unrighteousness in him.

PRINCIPLE 18:

We need worship songs that cause us to remember God's deeds that we would be glad, and sing for joy at his works.

Song 14: Songs Of Joy And Victory

Here's another lyric by an anonymous lyricist, Psalm 98. Its opening lines are the Biblical mandate for lyricists and songwriters and composers.

1 *O sing unto the Lord a new song;*
for he hath done marvellous things:
his right hand,
and his holy arm,
hath gotten him the victory.
2 *The Lord hath made known his salvation:*
his righteousness hath he openly shewed
in the sight of the heathen.
3 *He hath remembered his mercy*
and his truth toward the house of Israel:
all the ends of the earth have seen the salvation of our God.
4 *Make a joyful noise unto the Lord,*
all the earth:
make a loud noise,
and rejoice,
and sing praise.
5 *Sing unto the Lord with the harp;*
with the harp,
and the voice of a psalm.
6 *With trumpets and sound of cornet*
make a joyful noise before the Lord,
the King.
7 *Let the sea roar,*
and the fulness thereof;
the world, and they that dwell therein.
8 *Let the floods clap their hands:*
let the hills be joyful together
9 *Before the Lord;*
for he cometh to judge the earth:
with righteousness shall he judge the world,
and the people with equity.

Principle 19:

Marvelous things that happen deserve a song.

SONG 15: A PRAYER FOR DELIVERANCE FROM FALSE ACCUSERS

Psalm 120, which some think was written by Hezekiah, has a very astute lyric.

1 In my distress I cried unto the Lord,
and he heard me.
2 Deliver my soul, O Lord,
from lying lips,
and from a deceitful tongue.
3 What shall be given unto thee?
or what shall be done unto thee,
thou false tongue?
4 Sharp arrows of the mighty,
with coals of juniper.
5 Woe is me, that I sojourn in Mesech,
that I dwell in the tents of Kedar!
6 My soul hath long dwelt with him that hateth peace.
7 I am for peace:
but when I speak, they are for war.

The condition is spelled out in the last lines, here, from the NIV translation:

6 Too long have I lived
among those who hate peace.
7 I am a man of peace;
but when I speak, they are for war.

This lyric isn't just for political leaders. It can be with Christians in the middle of a dysfunctional family, a parent who's an alcoholic, a family member who's verbally abusive, etc.. It's this situation that prompts Hezekiah to write:

2 Save me, O Lord, from lying lips and from deceitful tongues.

The opening line tells us that this song is a call to God. Herein is our next principle.

PRINCIPLE 20

It's appropriate to write songs that call on the Lord in song when we're in distress and we are specific as to what the distress is about, in this case, being delivered from false accusers.

Song 16: The Vanity Of Laboring In Life Without God The Builder

Solomon, the lyricist of Psalm 127, tells us that if the Lord isn't the builder or the night guard, we work and watch in vain. This type of song reminds us of the vanity of working merely in our own strength. God is our co-laborer. He's our co-builder, our co-night guard. The song reminds us of the vanity of getting up early and staying up late. Again, this points to the vanity of doing it in our own strength. The closest pop song to this idea is Gordon Lightfoot's *The Cat's In the Cradle*, about a Dad who was too busy and a son who grew up to be just like him.

1 Except the Lord build the house,
they labour in vain that build it:
except the Lord keep the city,
the watchman waketh but in vain.
2 It is vain for you to rise up early,
to sit up late, to eat the bread of sorrows:
for so he giveth his beloved sleep.
3 Lo, children are an heritage of the Lord:
and the fruit of the womb is his reward.
4 As arrows are in the hand of a mighty man;
so are children of the youth.
5 Happy is the man that hath his quiver full of them:
they shall not be ashamed,
but they shall speak with the enemies in the gate.

Principle 21:

It's appropriate to write songs that remind us of the correct priorities of life and the vanity of building that life without God as our partner.

SONG 17: THE MARRIAGE SONG SUNG BY A PROFESSIONAL SINGER

Psalm 128 is a unique song because it was often sung at Israelite marriages. So now we have yet another wedding song, but this time sung by a singer and not the couple. The purpose of this song is to grant a blessing on the new union.

1 Blessed is every one that feareth the Lord;
that walketh in his ways.
2 For thou shalt eat the labour of thine hands:
happy shalt thou be,
and it shall be well with thee.
3 Thy wife shall be as a fruitful vine
by the sides of thine house:
thy children like olive plants
round about thy table.
4 Behold, that thus shall the man be blessed
that feareth the Lord.
5 The Lord shall bless thee out of Zion:
and thou shalt see the good of Jerusalem
all the days of thy life.
6 Yea, thou shalt see thy children's children,
and peace upon Israel.

PRINCIPLE 22

It's appropriate to write songs that bless new marriages and encourage the growth of young families.

Song 18: The Confidence Song In The Face Of Oppression

Psalm 129 is a song of opposites given the tenor of Heman's song in Psalm 88. This is a fighting song.

1 Many a time
have they afflicted me from my youth,
may Israel now say:
2 Many a time
have they afflicted me from my youth:
yet they have not prevailed against me.
3 The plowers plowed upon my back:
they made long their furrows.
4 The Lord is righteous:
he hath cut asunder the cords of the wicked.
5 Let them all be confounded and turned back that hate Zion.
6 Let them be as the grass upon the housetops,
which withereth afore it groweth up:
7 Wherewith the mower filleth not his hand;
nor he that bindeth sheaves his bosom.
8 Neither do they which go by say,
"The blessing of the Lord be upon you:
we bless you in the name of the Lord."

Consider these lines, here, from the NIV translation:

2 they have greatly oppressed me from my youth,
but they have not gained the victory over me.
3 Plowmen have plowed my back and made their furrows long.
4 But the Lord is righteous,
he has cut me free from the cords of the wicked

Principle 23:

It's appropriate to write songs openly expressing our internal confidence that we will overcome because of God's deliverance.

SONG 19: THE ASSURANCE OF FORGIVENESS

Consider this lyric, Psalm 130, written by an anonymous songwriter. I believe this is a very important type of song because, very often, people don't think they're forgiven, or don't accept forgiveness, and so continue to punish themselves. Then there are those who don't even feel they need forgiveness, it's the other fellow's problem.

1 Out of the depths have I cried unto thee, O Lord.
2 Lord, hear my voice:
let thine ears be attentive
to the voice of my supplications.
3 If thou, Lord, shouldest mark iniquities,
O Lord, who shall stand?
4 But there is forgiveness with thee,
that thou mayest be feared.
5 I wait for the Lord,
my soul doth wait,
and in his word do I hope.
6 My soul waiteth for the Lord more than they that watch for the morning:
I say, more than they that watch for the morning.
7 Let Israel hope in the Lord:
for with the Lord there is mercy,
and with him is plenteous redemption.
8 And he shall redeem Israel from all his iniquities.

PRINCIPLE 24:

It's appropriate to write songs that remind us to accept, receive, and give forgiveness.

Song 20: Celebrating Good Relationships And Friendships

Psalm 133, written by David, is purely about the joy of good friendships in unity. It reflects that such unity in relationships is a blessing of God.

1 *Behold,*
how good and how pleasant it is
for brethren to dwell together in unity!
2 *It is like the precious ointment upon the head,*
that ran down upon the beard,
even Aaron's beard:
that went down to the skirts of his garments;
3 *As the dew of Hermon,*
and as the dew that descended upon the mountains of Zion:
for there the Lord commanded the blessing,
even life for evermore.

Principle 25

It's appropriate to write songs about healthy relationships from the Lord and the joy we have in them.

SONG 21: THE VICTORY SONG

This is an all out victory/celebration song to be sung in public. Psalm 149 tells us that we're to sing this new song in the presence of the saints, to praise his name with dancing, musical instruments, percussion, the works.

1 *Praise ye the Lord.*
Sing unto the Lord a new song,
and his praise in the congregation of saints.
2 *Let Israel rejoice in him that made him:*
let the children of Zion be joyful in their King.
3 *Let them praise his name in the dance:*
let them sing praises unto him with the timbrel and harp.
4 *For the Lord taketh pleasure in his people:*
he will beautify the meek with salvation.
5 *Let the saints be joyful in glory:*
let them sing aloud upon their beds.
6 *Let the high praises of God be in their mouth,*
and a two-edged sword in their hand;
7 *To execute vengeance upon the heathen,*
and punishments upon the people;
8 *To bind their kings with chains,*
and their nobles with fetters of iron;
9 *To execute upon them the judgment written:*
this honour have all his saints.
Praise ye the Lord.

SONG 22: THE PURE LOVE SONG

Song of Solomon, as correctly labeled, is a *shi'yr*, therefore a song with melody and musical accompaniment. It's written for a male and female vocalist, and a chorus. There is no performance information available about this work, but reading the lyric suggests that it might have been produced in a concert/stage format. Although we can't be sure. Also, a reading of the text suggests that within the Song there is a kind of ballet as the female singer runs to look for her lover.

As a song, how does *Song of Solomon* build and shape the soul?

I make my comments in light of three varying theological views that you'll need to evaluate for yourself. The first is that *Song of Solomon* is a marriage manual between the husband and wife. The second is that it's an allegory between Christ and the Church. The third, is that it's an extended, intimate love song, the production of which would most likely be a kind of opera, if produced within the Western music tradition.

THE FIRST VIEW

Is *Song of Solomon* a marriage manual? Yes, in the sense that the instruction is inferred and sung, but not didactically taught, which is what a manual does. Reading it in the NIV, God's name is not mentioned. Its total focus is on the emotions and language of love using symbolism within the Israelite culture. Whether it's a marriage manual is certainly up to the reader to decide. But, what we must consider of this canonized work is that it gives us a written verbal range of what God considers to be healthy intimate communication between a husband and wife. From a counseling perspective, we have a document that sets boundaries. Given the percentages of men and women in the church that have come out of sexually abusive backgrounds, *Song of Solomon* sets a communications standard. There's lots of room for expression, but there is a line.

Song of Solomon also sets a healthy standard for pop music. For example, in some hip hop/rap songs, women are frequently referred to as a "ho" (short for whore), accompanied with graphic language as to the type of physical relationship desired by the singer. When *Song of Solomon* is looked upon as a benchmark, we see how far society is straying from healthy love talk in song. One appropriate response from the Christian community would be to write better love songs.

Writing a good, healthy love song builds the body, and becomes salt and light to the world.

THE SECOND VIEW

The idea that *Song of Solomon* is an allegory between Christ and the Church, given the imagery and symbolism, has come about because many theologians are uncomfortable with the level of sexual intimacy expressed in this song. Yet, it's canonized. Perhaps it's wise to consider the words of Paul from Philippians 4:8 (NIV):

Finally, brothers, whatever is true, whatever is noble, whatever is right, whatever is pure, whatever is lovely, whatever is admirable - if anything is excellent or praiseworthy - think about such things.

Thus sits canonized in the Bible, *Song of Solomon*.

THE THIRD VIEW

The most cursory reading strongly suggests that this is a highly intimate love song. What sets the pace, and what is often ignored in commentaries on this book, is that the love language used here builds the lovers. The language never tears them down, and never denigrates or debases them. It's always encouraging and supporting.

CULTURAL CONSIDERATIONS

Imagery is cultural. Three millennia ago, it was clearly a compliment for Solomon to compare her teeth to a flock of sheep, "*coming up from the washing.*" (NIV). That imagery in an industrialized nation is strange, and out of place. Even so, the intent of the imagery is to build the other, thus fitting God's instruction through Paul about the purpose of music in the *ekklesia*.

Summation

In this section, we've looked at the uses of the word *shi'yr* for the different types of songs in the Bible. We've discovered 22 songs by content. There are probably several more. The difference between the secular song and God's music is that God is at the center of all. It's His handiwork that delivers us, blesses us, provides for us, marries us, give us children and a healthy sexual life in marriage. All are deemed worthy for song and public performance when tastefully written.

If we examine these 22 types of *shi'yrs* by content, in context, we see a wide variety of subjects on which to write and perform in public. The range of music is from reflective to shouting to intimate, instructional, and prophetic. Reflected are solo songs, duets, musicals, praise songs, and full choral works, from solo harp to full string ensemble, to full orchestra to 120 trumpeters.

We see music used as the great encourager to keep people focused in their relationship with God, to seek deliverance, blessings and then through music to praise the living God for his response and blessings. In fact, if we were to count them, we would probably find that most *shi'yrs* are songs requesting deliverance or about deliverance (i.e., being rescued).

Principle 26

God's lyrics are made up of songs of personal and emotional vulnerability publicly performed.

Principle 27

In one form or another, the purpose of God's music is to build. Even direct praise songs to God have a secondary training purpose of reminding the believer that God will not abandon him. Except for Song of Solomon which was performed separately, the mocking song, and the two wedding song types, 18 of the 22 shi'yr types were performed in the Temple.

STANDARDS AND PRACTICES

Here, then, I believe is part of the standard of training people in the art of creating music that worships the Lord.

1. We are to be an emotionally expressive and communicative people through the masterful use of vibrant, evocative, colorful, vivid, symbolic and imaginative words in music and, as we'll later see, with instrumental music alone.
2. The music and words can cover the full range of life with God at its center.
3. We're to be competent in the public performance of that music. This last point flies in the face of those who fear that too polished a performance focuses on the performer and not on God.
4. 21 of the 22 types represent the kinds of lyrics to feed our *nephesh* (soul), through encouragement, warning or emotional release.
5. As appointed music leaders, our tools are words, principles of harmony and counterpoint, and orchestration for singers and instruments.

APPLICATION TO THE CHRISTIAN ARTIST & SONGWRITER/LYRICIST

From the content of this chapter, here's a proposed definition of what a Christian artist, songwriter or lyricist is:

> *A Christian artist, songwriter or lyricist, is a person, appointed by God, who makes themselves vulnerable by way of public performance for proclaiming both the faith struggles and the historic acts of God's deliverance in their personal life and daily walk with God.*

Chapter 5

Thanks & The 3 Types Of Praise Songs

There's one song type for *thanksgiving/testify* and three different song types for *praise*. Each type started first as a word describing an action or human response in relationship with God or another individual. Then, in the Israelite culture, that action/response became a type of praise song that's not locked into any particular music style. The key is to see how these words are used in relationship with each other so that we understand how we use them in song in our relationship with God.

Defining Our Terms

The four words are:

- **Yadah -** *testify, confess*
- **Halal -** *boast, shout, praise*
- **Barak -** *blessing, a dropping to one knee*
- **Tehilla -** *praise, a specific type of song or hymn whose style is lost to us*

In this chapter, we'll look at each song type with an example of each.

Yadah

Pronounced *yaw-daw*. This word is most often translated *thanksgiving* in the NIV. As a word, the first verse we see *yadah* used in is Genesis 29:35.

And she conceived again, and bare a son: and she said, Now will I ***praise*** *[yadah] the LORD: therefore she called his name Judah; and left bearing.*

Another use is in Leviticus 5:5,

And it shall be, when he shall be guilty in one of these things, that he shall ***confess*** *[yadah] that he hath sinned in that thing:*

One of the first places we see praise in a corporate setting is in I Chronicles 16:4. Here David has brought back the Ark of the Covenant. He's assigned Levites to do some very specific tasks.

He appointed some of the Levites to minister before the ark of the Lord, to make petition, to give thanks, and to praise the Lord, the God of Israel: (I Chron. 16:4, NIV)

The three tasks are:

1. To make petition
2. To give thanks
3. To praise the Lord

Our concern is over the thanks and the praise. When we look up the words, we see that thanks is *yadah*, a public acknowledgment, and praise is *halal*, a shout of victory. If we expand out the translation, we get this insight.

David appointed some of the Levites to minister before the ark of the Lord to make petitions (remembrances), to give public acknowledgment of all that the Lord had done, and to shout and rave about the Lord, the God of Israel.

Now, if we're going to properly train people in the art of music for worship, we should know what a *yadah* is. This way we can properly instruct songwriters, lyricists and composers in what they should write and score. We find the answer in I Chronicles 16:7 (NIV):

That day David first committed to Asaph and his associates this psalm of thanks to the Lord:

From verses 8 to 36, we have a complete psalm of *yadah*, a lyric read to musical accompaniment that gives God public acknowledgment. Here it is, the only surviving *yadah* in the Bible that we're aware of, found in I Chronicles 16:8-36 (NIV).

8 Give thanks to the LORD, call on his name;
make known among the nations what he has done.
9 Sing to him, sing praise to him;
tell of all his wonderful acts.
10 Glory in his holy name;
let the hearts of those who seek the LORD rejoice.
11 Look to the LORD and his strength;
seek his face always.
12 Remember the wonders he has done,
his miracles, and the judgments he pronounced,
13 O descendants of Israel his servant,
O sons of Jacob, his chosen ones.
14 He is the LORD our God;
his judgments are in all the earth.
15 He remembers his covenant forever,
the word he commanded,
for a thousand generations,
16 the covenant he made with Abraham,
the oath he swore to Isaac.
17 He confirmed it to Jacob as a decree,
to Israel as an everlasting covenant:
18 "To you I will give the land of Canaan
as the portion you will inherit."
19 When they were but few in number,
few indeed, and strangers in it,
20 they wandered from nation to nation,
from one kingdom to another.
21 He allowed no man to oppress them;
for their sake he rebuked kings:
22 "Do not touch my anointed ones;
do my prophets no harm."

23 Sing to the LORD, all the earth;
proclaim his salvation day after day.
24 Declare his glory among the nations,
his marvelous deeds among all peoples.
25 For great is the LORD and most worthy of praise;
he is to be feared above all gods.
26 For all the gods of the nations are idols,
but the LORD made the heavens.
27 Splendor and majesty are before him;
strength and joy in his dwelling place.

28 *Ascribe to the LORD, O families of nations,*
ascribe to the LORD glory and strength,
29 *ascribe to the LORD the glory due his name.*
Bring an offering and come before him;
worship the LORD in the splendor of his holiness.
30 *Tremble before him, all the earth!*
The world is firmly established;
it cannot be moved.
31 *Let the heavens rejoice,*
let the earth be glad;
let them say among the nations, "The LORD reigns!"
32 *Let the sea resound,*
and all that is in it;
let the fields be jubilant,
and everything in them!
33 *Then the trees of the forest will sing,*
they will sing for joy before the LORD,
for he comes to judge the earth.

34 *Give thanks to the LORD, for he is good;*
his love endures forever.
35 *Cry out, "Save us, O God our Savior;*
gather us and deliver us from the nations,
that we may give thanks to your holy name,
that we may glory in your praise.
36 *"Praise be to the LORD, the God of Israel,*
from everlasting to everlasting."

HOW THE YADAH IS CONSTRUCTED

Now, I've broken this *yadah* into three sections. This may not be the natural break in the Psalm, but scholarly detective work has discovered that each of these three sections are contained in other Psalms. Here's the breakdown of parallels according to the *Bible Knowledge Commentary*:

I Chronicles	**Psalms**
16: 8-22	105: 1-15
16: 23-33	96: 1b-13a
16: 34-36	106: 1b-c, 47-48

Most of the commentaries suggest that David created this Psalm by pulling from three other Psalms he had written and then editing the pieces together. That's certainly a possibility, but as a composer, I can tell you that's the long way to go. Perhaps there's another view that scholars, not being professional lyric writers, have missed, which is that David created this work first, and later excerpted from it into the three smaller ones.

It's very much a problem/solution thing.

You're in the middle of a piece and you realize that something you wrote earlier, perhaps a theme, fits this new situation perfectly, so you borrow from that earlier work. Or you created a theme you like quite a bit, and now you want to develop it and take it in a different direction. I see that principle could be at work here, too.

PERMISSION SLIPS

Regardless, as writers we now have a permission slip or two. Because it's done in the Bible, now we can take complementing passages from other portions of Scripture and put them together to create a new psalm or song. Since David did it, it's also permissible to borrow from our own earlier works to develop the themes or apply them where there's an appropriate match up.

FORM BY CONTENT

1. First theme is a call to praise (1-13)
2. Second theme is a summation of deliverance (14-22)
3. Third theme is an acknowledgment of being saved by praising God's attributes (23-33)
4. Fourth theme is an affirmation that we can call on God to save us (34-35)
5. Fifth theme is a summation of praise to God (36)

You can do further analysis by looking at each pair of lines and seeing what type of parallelism they represent. Armed with this information, you have the basis for creating a whole new set of songs of *yadah*.

Our suggested form by content would be ABCDA^1 with A^1 being verse 36. So musically, the challenge is to create four different musical feels for each section and then the wrap up verse.

HALAL

Pronounced *hah-lal*. I've defined this as a victory shout or rave. It can also mean to shine, to boast about, to praise. An *halal* can be a short, two line phrase sung repeatedly, Or it can be a longer work.

HOW THE WORD HALAL IS USED

It's used 140 times in the Old Testament. Its first use is in Genesis 12:15:

The princes also of Pharaoh saw her, and ***commended*** *[halal] her before Pharaoh: and the woman was taken into Pharaoh's house.*

It's used to describe David feigning madness before the Philistines in I Samuel 21:13:

And he changed his behaviour before them, and ***feigned himself mad*** *[halal] in their hands, and scrabbled on the doors of the gate, and let his spittle fall down upon his beard.*

It's used to describe Absalom and his handsomeness in II Samuel 14:25:

But in all Israel there was none to be so much ***praised*** *[halal] as Absalom for his beauty: from the sole of his foot even to the crown of his head there was no blemish in him.*

In Proverbs 27:1-2 it's used to warn about the dangers of self-praise:

Boast *[halal] not thyself of tomorrow; for thou knowest not what a day may bring forth. Let another man* ***praise*** *[halal] thee, and not thine own mouth; a stranger, and not thine own lips.*

In Proverbs 31:30-31 it speaks of how a Godly wife is praised:

Favour is deceitful, and beauty is vain: but a woman that feareth the LORD, she shall be ***praised*** *[halal]. Give her of the fruit of her hands; and let her own works* ***praise*** *[halal] her in the gates.*

FOR CORPORATE PRAISE

In I Chronicles, David gives instruction for using the *halal* corporately. The instructions were to *halal* in the morning and in the evening.

And he appointed certain of the Levites to minister before the ark of the LORD, and to record, and to thank and ***praise*** *[halal] the LORD God of Israel:* (I Chronicles 16:4)

Moreover four thousand were porters; and four thousand ***praised*** *[halal] the LORD with the instruments which I made, said David, to* ***praise*** *[halal] therewith.* (I Chronicles 23:5)

And to stand every morning to thank and ***praise*** *[halal] the LORD, and likewise at even;* (I Chronicles 23:30)

TOWARDS GOD

In the Psalms, we see these points within the lyrics, but then we see how we're to *halal* God:

In God we ***boast*** *[halal] all the day long, and* ***praise*** *[halal] thy name for ever. Selah.* (Psalms 44:8)

For the LORD is great, and greatly to be ***praised*** *[halal]: he is to be feared above all gods.* (Psalms 96:4)

Praise *[halal] ye the LORD. I will* ***praise*** *[halal] the LORD with my whole heart, in the assembly of the upright, and in the congregation.* (Psalms 111:1)

THE HALAL PRAISE CHORUS

In II Chronicles 5:13-14, NIV, we find this:

The trumpeters and singers joined in unison, as with one voice, to give ***praise*** *[halal] and* ***thanks*** *[yadah] to the Lord. Accompanied by trumpets, cymbals and other instruments, they raised their voices in praise to the Lord and sang:*

"He is good,
his love endures forever."

Then the temple of the Lord was filled with a cloud and the priests could not perform their service because of the cloud, for the glory of the Lord filled the temple of God.

This two-line verse is an *halal*. It functions like a praise chorus continually repeated with singing and victory shouts. The result was that the cloud of the glory of the Lord filled the service. This, then, is a picture of how God inhabits the praises (halals) of his people. Thus, very active, "boisterous" songs have a Biblical place when the *ekklesia* gathers. Note God's response when the people are sincere and in unity.

THE HALAL PSALMS

There are a second class of *halals*, what the Psalm translators call the *Halal Psalms*. These are expanded *halals* from which we learn more about how to lyrically shout about the Lord.

Psalms 113-118 are called the *Egyptian Halal* collection because they were mostly sung at the Passover. Some scholars believe they were written by Moses. Psalms 146-150, according to Dr. Peter C. Craigie, author of *Psalms 1-50 Word Commentary Series*, were used in general worship.

I'll leave these for you to read and study on your own, but the one psalm I do want to call attention to is Psalm 118. It's first verse reads:

Give thanks to the Lord, for he is good, his love endures forever. (NIV)

In Psalm 118 we have an entire *halal* psalm expanded out from the *halal* chorus sung in the service celebrating the return of the Ark of Covenant. Scholars agree that Psalm 118 is a military victory song.

Could it be possible that Psalm 118 is the complete *halal* psalm sung that day before the Ark of the Covenant?

Its content certainly suggests that. And if this is the case, then we have a glorious musical picture of that day of both a song of *yadah*, a *halal*, and a complete *halal* praise song.

Psalm 118

1 O give thanks unto the LORD; for he is good:
because his mercy endureth for ever.

2 Let Israel now say,
that his mercy endureth for ever.

3 Let the house of Aaron now say,
that his mercy endureth for ever.

4 Let them now that fear the LORD say,
that his mercy endureth for ever.

5 I called upon the LORD in distress:
the LORD answered me, and set me in a large place.
6 The LORD is on my side;
I will not fear:
what can man do unto me?
7 The LORD taketh my part with them that help me:
therefore shall I see my desire upon them that hate me.
8 It is better to trust in the LORD '
than to put confidence in man.
9 It is better to trust in the LORD
than to put confidence in princes.

10 All nations compassed me about:
but in the name of the LORD will I destroy them.
11 They compassed me about;
yea, they compassed me about:
but in the name of the LORD I will destroy them.
12 They compassed me about like bees;
they are quenched as the fire of thorns:
for in the name of the LORD I will destroy them.

13 Thou hast thrust sore at me that I might fall:
but the LORD helped me.
14 The LORD is my strength and song,
and is become my salvation.
15 The voice of rejoicing and salvation is in the tabernacles of the righteous:
the right hand of the LORD doeth valiantly.
16 The right hand of the LORD is exalted:
the right hand of the LORD doeth valiantly.
17 I shall not die, but live,
and declare the works of the LORD.

[18]The LORD hath chastened me sore:
but he hath not given me over unto death.

[19]Open to me the gates of righteousness:
I will go into them,
and I will praise the LORD:
[20]This gate of the LORD,
into which the righteous shall enter.
[21]I will praise thee:
for thou hast heard me, and art become my salvation.

[22]The stone which the builders refused is become the head stone of the corner.
[23]This is the LORD'S doing;
it is marvellous in our eyes.

[24]This is the day which the LORD hath made;
we will rejoice and be glad in it.

[25]Save now, I beseech thee, O LORD:
O LORD, I beseech thee,
send now prosperity.
[26]Blessed be he that cometh in the name of the LORD:
we have blessed you out of the house of the LORD.

[27]God is the LORD, which hath shewed us light:
bind the sacrifice with cords, even unto the horns of the altar.
[28]Thou art my God, and I will praise thee:
thou art my God, I will exalt thee.
[29]O give thanks unto the LORD;
for he is good:
for his mercy endureth for ever.

BARAK

Pronounced *bay-rak*. It means *to bless, to kneel* (bend the knee). The idea of bending the knee is the root concept of what Biblical humility is. To be humble is to bend the knee. It's used 289 times in the Old Testament.

If there was a song of *barak*, of blessing, I couldn't find one. The only possible exception is the blessing found in Numbers 6:24-26 (NIV). I've broken the verse into more songlike phrases.

The Lord bless you and keep you;
the Lord make his face
shine upon you
and be gracious to you;
the Lord turn his face toward you
and give you peace.

And we can certainly use this blessing as a model to write new blessings to the Lord to each other.

What we do find throughout the Psalms is the command to bless the Lord. The first use of the word *bless* is found in Genesis 1:22, where it says that God blessed (*barak*) Adam and Eve. As God blesses us, so do we bless God in our praises.

TEHILLAH

Tehillah is a *praise*, or *a song or hymn of praise*. It's used 46 times in the Old Testament. It's first use is in Exodus 15:11:

Who is like unto thee, O LORD, among the gods? who is like thee, glorious in holiness, fearful in ***praises*** *[tehillah], doing wonders?*

So, we now have a clue that a *tehillah* is a song that recites the great and awesome wonders God has done that we've seen with our own eyes.

Now, from Nehemiah 12:46 (NIV) we have this observation:

For long ago, in the days of David and Asaph, there had been directors for the singers and for the songs of ***praise*** *and* ***thanksgiving*** *to God.*

Thanksgiving is *yadah*. But what about a song of *tehillah*? Well, as it turns out, like the *yadah*, we only have one example of a song of *tehillah* and it's Psalm 145 (NIV).

A PSALM OF TEHILLAH. OF DAVID.

1 I will exalt you, my God the King;
I will praise your name for ever and ever.
2 Every day I will praise you
and extol your name for ever and ever.
3 Great is the LORD and most worthy of praise;
his greatness no one can fathom.

4 One generation will commend your works to another;
they will tell of your mighty acts.
5 They will speak of the glorious splendor of your majesty,
and I will meditate on your wonderful works.
6 They will tell of the power of your awesome works,
and I will proclaim your great deeds.
7 They will celebrate your abundant goodness and joyfully
sing of your righteousness.
8 The LORD is gracious and compassionate,
slow to anger and rich in love.
9 The LORD is good to all;
he has compassion on all he has made.

10 All you have made will praise you, O LORD,
your saints will extol you.
11 They will tell of the glory of your kingdom
and speak of your might,
12 so that all men may know of your mighty acts
and the glorious splendor of your kingdom.
13 Your kingdom is an everlasting kingdom,
and your dominion endures through all generations.

The LORD is faithful to all his promises
and loving toward all he has made.
14 The LORD upholds all those who fall and
lifts up all who are bowed down.
15 The eyes of all look to you,
and you give them their food at the proper time.
16 You open your hand
and satisfy the desires of every living thing.

17 *The LORD is righteous in all his ways*
and loving toward all he has made.
18 *The LORD is near to all who call on him,*
to all who call on him in truth.
19 *He fulfills the desires of those who fear him;*
he hears their cry and saves them.
20 *The LORD watches over all who love him,*
but all the wicked he will destroy.

21 *My mouth will speak in praise of the LORD.*
Let every creature praise his holy name for ever and ever.

HOW THIS SONG OF TEHILLAH IS CONSTRUCTED

Since Psalm 145 is the only *Song of Tehillah* we know of, we have to be careful at saying that this is how all songs of *tehillah* should be written. But we at least have some clues from Dr. Leslie C. Allen, professor of Old Testament at Fuller Theological Seminary from his book *Psalms 101;150* in the *Word Biblical Commentary series*.

AN ACROSTIC

First, what's lost to us in an English translation is that Psalm 145 is an acrostic, meaning that the first line of the song starts with a letter of the Hebrew alphabet. So now we have a lyric writing device, regardless of our language, we can create new songs with acrostics as the starting point for lyric creation. We can use the whole alphabet of our language, or apply the principle by creating a lyric from an acrostic of other words. Dr. Allen says this about the lyric:

It is marked by skillful artistry, especially discernible in its acrostic form, of which the poet was a master weaving its elegance neatly into the development of his thought.

I've underlined the comment, *"of which the poet was a master,"* to further demonstrate what I believe to be God's expectation of us in the arts to be the best at what we do, and that when we surrender ourselves to God, God works through our skills in ways greater than we can imagine. The more complete our surrender, along with the more highly developed skills we have, the more God works through us.

FORM AND ORGANIZATION

Second, is the organization or form of the psalm. In music, form, as defined by well known theorist Heinrich Schenker, is how you handle repeats. I've used Dr. Allen's breakdown with the NIV translation to show you Psalm 145's form. Here, the form is organized not by verses and choruses as we know them to be used in most pop/ rock music, but rather, by content.

As Dr. Allen explains, the song form by content is ABA^1B^1.

The psalm is in two broad sections, verses 1-9 and 10 to the end, There is a smaller structure, within the psalm where each section is broken in half, so that musically, we might say there are four musical verses. To understand this better, read verse 1-3 (A), then verses 10-13a (A^1). Then read verses 4-7 (B), and then 13b to the end (B^1). Musically, we could create two different themes, A and B so that the musical themes would work with the form by content, thus creating a musical whole.

I've taken a writer's liberty which is to separate the last line of Psalm 145 from all the rest. As a writer, this strikes me as the summation, the line on which I might be tempted to write a musical chorus for the congregation to repeat over and over. What kind of music is apropos? In the NIV, the feel is for a *halal*, Yet, in looking up this line, I see that the first use of praise is *tehillah*, and the second is *barak*, to bless, to bend the knee, to extol.

So as a composer, I'm compelled to look up each word for praise in a psalm so that as a Chief Musician, it's clear to me what type of music is needed to create the emotional under structure intended by the lyricist, in this case, David. So as a composer, I need a repeatable theme that both portrays God's awesome works and blesses him at the same time.

Here, we see the need for the Chief Musician to understand the elements of dramatic scoring in various instrumental combinations to bring out the lyricist's intentions (in this case, David) in this song.

MULTIPLE HEBREW NAMES FOR GOD

Third, the Psalmist uses multiple names of God to focus his praise. In the NIV version, God is *ELOHIM*; Lord is *Yahweh* in Dr. Allen's translation and *Jehovah* in QuickVerse.

FREEDOM TO CREATE NEW SONG FORMS

Fourth, we have the freedom to create new song structures. At the dawn of the 21st Century, most Christian music is constructed around the standard song forms (most frequently the pop/rock verse-chorus format), the praise song, and the standard church hymn. Now we have Biblical options. We're not stuck with the musical same old/same old. We have Biblical permission to expand to new musical and lyrical horizons and not remain stuck with the same tried and true formulas of the past. We have a creative God who expects us to create.

So what we have is a song with a tightly woven structure to it, created by a craftsman empowered by God, that speaks to us 2,800 years after it was written.

THE POWER OF COMBINING A HALAL AND A SONG OF TEHILLAH

If there are two kinds of praise songs teamed together that get results they are the *halal's* variant the *chalal* used with the *tehillah*. Consider this story from II Chronicles 20:22 (NIV), of King Jehoshaphat.

As they began to sing and praise, the Lord set ambushes against the men of Ammon and Moab and Mount Seir who were invading Judah and they were defeated.

On their way to battle in the Desert of Tekoa, Jehoshaphat appoints a group of men to sing while walking ahead of the army (in military terms, this would be considered *walking point*). Any soldier who's ever taken the point knows that you don't sing. You keep deadly quiet and walk ahead to recon the situation and report back, not infrequently looking for booby traps.

Not here!

Instead, the men taking the point position sang a *chalal* and *tehillah*. To *chalal* is *to shout with a creaking sound*. So the Israelite army march and shouted with a creaking voice (one can only imagine what that sounded like!) and they praised the Lord with a *tehillah*. The *chalal* they sang is a modification of the one sung on the day of the temple dedication:

Give thanks to the Lord,
for his love endures forever. (II Chronicles 20:21, NIV)

So now we have two *halals*: one sung in the temple, the other in battle. While I'm sure *halals* could be on various subjects, the two we have, in their second line, focus on the fact that God's love endures forever. Perhaps we have here a formula to consider for writing new *halals*.

WE ARE TO BE A TEHILLAH OF GOD

Then we have this interesting second use of the word *tehillah* in Deuteronomy 26:19 (NIV):

He has declared that he will set you in praise,
fame and honor high above all the nations he has made
and that you will be a people holy to the Lord your God,
as he promised.

The word for praise is *tehillah*. The earthly result of obedience is that God will set us in *tehillah*, fame and honor above all others. In other words, God will praise us for the great and awesome wonders that we do in obedience to him in fulfillment of our mission.

WRAP UP

For the *halal*, the *yadah*, the *barak*, and the *tehillah*, we now have one example of each within Scripture. We know they were sung, performed with instruments, recited with instrumental backup, and were often loud, brassy and shouting.

We close with two important observations:

First, having identified each of the four types and each with one model, we can now begin creating new Biblically driven thanksgiving and praise songs in any language or music style by applying the lyric principles contained within each type. The implications of this for missions outside the United States are enormous for helping whole tribes and cultures, in obedience to Scripture, create their own new praise and worship music following the Biblical models.

Second, we have clear tangible demonstrations of what happens in the lives of worshippers or an army in battle when, with their whole hearts, they *halal* and *yadah* the Lord, or *chalal* and *tehillah* the Lord.

CHAPTER 6

8 MORE TYPES OF BIBLICAL SONGS

Within the Psalms, we find eight more song types. Historically, we have very little information about them and their performance, although we do know what the Hebrew words mean. For this chapter, I interviewed Dr. Leslie Allen of Fuller Theological Seminary (author of two Word Commentaries on the Psalms). I also consulted Dr. Peter Craigie's book on the Psalms. The information in this chapter is summarized from those Word Commentaries and is presented for those who want to go deeper.

- **Maskil -** *an instructive didactic lyric*
- **Zakar -** *to remember, a song of remembrance*
- **Miktam -** *a secret*
- **Tephillah -** *a prayer written as a song lyric*
- **Songs of Ascents -** *a collection of songs for Passover*
- **Shiggaion -** *a song of errors*
- **Qinah -** *a song of crisis*
- **Todah -** *a song of resolution after the crisis is over* (often sung in pairs with the *Qinah*)

MASKIL

There are 13 *maskils* in the Psalms. A maskil is an instructive didactic lyric whose purpose is *to instruct or cause reflection*. These are Psalms 32, 42, 44, 45, 52-55, 74, 78, 88-89, 142. We'll consider Psalm 42.

According to Dr. Craigie, Psalms 42-43 form a single unit. It falls into three sections:

1. 42:1-5 (a) Lament (1-4) (b) Refrain (5)
2. 42:6-11 (a) Lament (6-10) (b) Refrain (11)
3. 43:1-5 (a) Prayer (1-4) (b) Refrain (5)

The form of this *maskil* is very close to our modern verse-chorus song form.

1 As the hart panteth after the water brooks,
so panteth my soul after thee, O God.
2 My soul thirsteth for God,
for the living God:
when shall I come and appear before God?
3 My tears have been my meat day and night,
while they continually say unto me, "Where is thy God?"
4 When I remember these things,
I pour out my soul in me:
for I had gone with the multitude,
I went with them to the house of God,
with the voice of joy and praise,
with a multitude that kept holyday.

5 Why art thou cast down, O my soul?
and why art thou disquieted in me?
hope thou in God:
for I shall yet praise him
for the help of his countenance.

6 O my God,
my soul is cast down within me:
therefore will I remember thee
from the land of Jordan,
and of the Hermonites,
from the hill Mizar.
7 Deep calleth unto deep
at the noise of thy waterspouts:
all thy waves and thy billows
are gone over me.
8 Yet the Lord will command his lovingkindness in the daytime,
and in the night his song shall be with me,
and my prayer unto the God of my life.
9 I will say unto God my rock,
"Why hast thou forgotten me?
why go I mourning because of the oppression of the enemy?
10 As with a sword in my bones,
mine enemies reproach me;
while they say daily unto me,
'Where is thy God?'"

11 Why art thou cast down, O my soul?
and why art thou disquieted within me?
hope thou in God: for I shall yet praise him,
who is the health of my countenance, and my God.

[1] Judge me, O God,
and plead my cause against an ungodly nation:
O deliver me from the deceitful and unjust man.
[2] For thou art the God of my strength:
why dost thou cast me off?
why go I mourning
because of the oppression of the enemy?
[3] O send out thy light and thy truth:
let them lead me;
let them bring me unto thy holy hill,
and to thy tabernacles.
[4] Then will I go unto the altar of God,
unto God my exceeding joy:
yea, upon the harp will I praise thee, O God my God.

[5] Why art thou cast down, O my soul?
and why art thou disquieted within me?
hope in God:
for I shall yet praise him,
who is the health of my countenance,
and my God.

Zakar

A *zakar* is a *petition*, a *remembrance*. Its first use is in Genesis 8:1

And God **remembered** *[zakar] Noah, and every living thing, and all the cattle that was with him in the ark: and God made a wind to pass over the earth, and the waters asswaged;*

The two *zakar* Psalms are 38 and 70. Below is Psalm 70.

[1] Make haste, O God, to deliver me;
make haste to help me, O Lord.
[2] Let them be ashamed and confounded that seek after my soul:
let them be turned backward, and put to confusion,
that desire my hurt.
[3] Let them be turned back for a reward of their shame that say, Aha, aha.
[4] Let all those that seek thee rejoice and be glad in thee:
and let such as love thy salvation say continually, Let God be magnified.
[5] But I am poor and needy:
make haste unto me, O God:
thou art my help and my deliverer;
O Lord, make no tarrying.

MIKTAM

A *miktam* is a *secret*, a *song with deep import*. The word is only found in the Psalms and there are six of them: 16, 56-60. We'll consider Dr. Craigie's outline for Psalm 16.

1.	Introduction	verse 1
2.	Words of an acquaintance	2-4a
3.	Song of confidence	4b-11

1 *Preserve me, O God:*
for in thee do I put my trust.

2 *O my soul, thou hast said unto the Lord,*
Thou art my Lord:
my goodness extendeth not to thee;
3 *But to the saints that are in the earth,*
and to the excellent,
in whom is all my delight.
4a *Their sorrows shall be multiplied that hasten after another god:*

4b *their drink offerings of blood will I not offer,*
nor take up their names into my lips.
5 *The Lord is the portion of mine inheritance and of my cup:*
thou maintainest my lot.
6 *The lines are fallen unto me in pleasant places;*
yea, I have a goodly heritage.
7 *I will bless the Lord, who hath given me counsel:*
my reins also instruct me in the night seasons.
8 *I have set the Lord always before me:*
because he is at my right hand,
I shall not be moved.
9 *Therefore my heart is glad,*
and my glory rejoiceth:
my flesh also shall rest in hope.
10 *For thou wilt not leave my soul in hell;*
neither wilt thou suffer thine Holy One to see corruption.
11 *Thou wilt shew me the path of life:*
in thy presence is fulness of joy;
at thy right hand there are pleasures for evermore.

Tephillah

A *tephillah* is an *intercessory prayer*, and it's used 70 times in the Old Testament. The word is used in relationship to the act of praying a specific prayer to God, and for God to announce that he has heard the *tephillah*. It's first used in II Samuel 7:27.

For thou, O LORD of hosts, God of Israel, hast revealed to thy servant, saying, I will build thee an house: therefore hath thy servant found in his heart to pray this ***prayer*** *[tephillah] unto thee.*

There are psalms where the writer asks for his *tephillah* to be heard. Some examples are Psalms 55, 66, and 142.

There are four prayers in the Psalms that have been set to music: 17, 90, 102, 143. Below is Psalm 17.

1 *Hear the right, O Lord, attend unto my cry,*
give ear unto my prayer, that goeth not out of feigned lips.
2 *Let my sentence come forth from thy presence;*
let thine eyes behold the things that are equal.

3 *Thou hast proved mine heart;*
thou hast visited me in the night;
thou hast tried me, and shalt find nothing;
I am purposed that my mouth shall not transgress.
4 *Concerning the words of men,*
by the word of thy lips
I have kept me from the paths of the destroyer.
5 *Hold up my goings in thy paths,*
that my footsteps slip not.

6 *I have called upon thee, for thou wilt hear me, O God:*
incline thine ear unto me, and hear my speech.
7 *Shew thy marvellous lovingkindness,*
O thou that savest by thy right hand them which put their trust in thee
from those that rise up against them.
8 *Keep me as the apple of the eye,*
hide me under the shadow of thy wings,
9 *From the wicked that oppress me,*
from my deadly enemies, who compass me about.
10 *They are inclosed in their own fat:*
with their mouth they speak proudly.
11 *They have now compassed us in our steps:*

they have set their eyes bowing down to the earth;
12 *Like as a lion that is greedy of his prey,*
and as it were a young lion lurking in secret places.

13 *Arise, O Lord,*
disappoint him, cast him down:
deliver my soul from the wicked, which is thy sword:
14 *From men which are thy hand, O Lord,*
from men of the world, which have their portion in this life,
and whose belly thou fillest with thy hid treasure:
they are full of children,
and leave the rest of their substance to their babes.
15 *As for me, I will behold thy face in righteousness:*
I shall be satisfied, when I awake, with thy likeness.

SONGS OF ASCENTS

Songs of Ascents or *ma'alah* are, apparently, a special type of song. *Ascent* means *thoughts that go up*. We have a group of them. Psalms 120-134. They were sung before and after the Jewish festivals, especially the Feast of Tabernacles. Below is Psalm 120. It's repeated here for consistency.

1 *In my distress I cried unto the Lord, and he heard me.*
2 *Deliver my soul, O Lord, from lying lips, and from a deceitful tongue.*
3 *What shall be given unto thee? or what shall be done unto thee, thou false tongue?*
4 *Sharp arrows of the mighty, with coals of juniper.*
5 *Woe is me, that I sojourn in Mesech, that I dwell in the tents of Kedar!*
6 *My soul hath long dwelt with him that hateth peace.*
7 *I am for peace: but when I speak, they are for war.*

Shiggaion

A *shiggaion* is a *song of errors* or a *rambling song*. We have one in Psalm 7.

1 *O Lord my God,*
in thee do I put my trust:
save me from all them that persecute me, and deliver me:
2 *Lest he tear my soul like a lion,*
rending it in pieces, while there is none to deliver.
3 *O Lord my God,*
if I have done this;
if there be iniquity in my hands;
4 *If I have rewarded evil unto him that was at peace with me;*
(yea, I have delivered him that without cause is mine enemy:)
5 *Let the enemy persecute my soul, and take it;*
yea, let him tread down my life upon the earth,
and lay mine honour in the dust. Selah.
6 *Arise, O Lord, in thine anger,*
lift up thyself because of the rage of mine enemies:
and awake for me to the judgment that thou hast commanded.
7 *So shall the congregation of the people compass thee about:*
for their sakes therefore return thou on high.
8 *The Lord shall judge the people:*
judge me, O Lord, according to my righteousness,
and according to mine integrity that is in me.
9 *Oh let the wickedness of the wicked come to an end;*
but establish the just:
for the righteous God trieth the hearts and reins.
10 *My defence is of God,*
which saveth the upright in heart.
11 *God judgeth the righteous,*
and God is angry with the wicked every day.
12 *If he turn not, he will whet his sword;*
he hath bent his bow, and made it ready.
13 *He hath also prepared for him the instruments of death;*
he ordaineth his arrows against the persecutors.
14 *Behold, he travaileth with iniquity,*
and hath conceived mischief,
and brought forth falsehood.
15 *He made a pit, and digged it,*
and is fallen into the ditch which he made.
16 *His mischief shall return upon his own head,*
and his violent dealing shall come down upon his own pate.
17 *I will praise the Lord according to his righteousness:*
and will sing praise to the name of the Lord most high.

QINAH

The *qinah* and the *todah* are best performed in pairs. That's because the *qinah* is our *song of lament or complaint* to God while we're experiencing difficulty, while the *todah* is God's *resolution*. Psalm 6 is an example of the *qinah*. According to Dr. Peter C. Craigie, it's in three parts. Here's the outline:

cry of anguish	1-3
a prayer for deliverance from misery	4-7
confidence in answered prayer	8-10

PSALM 6

1 *O Lord, rebuke me not in thine anger,*
neither chasten me in thy hot displeasure.
2 *Have mercy upon me, O Lord;*
for I am weak: O Lord, heal me;
for my bones are vexed.
3 *My soul is also sore vexed:*
but thou, O Lord, how long?

4 *Return, O Lord, deliver my soul:*
oh save me for thy mercies' sake.
5 *For in death there is no remembrance of thee:*
in the grave who shall give thee thanks?
6 *I am weary with my groaning;*
all the night make I my bed to swim;
I water my couch with my tears.
7 *Mine eye is consumed because of grief;*
it waxeth old because of all mine enemies.

8 *Depart from me, all ye workers of iniquity;*
for the Lord hath heard the voice of my weeping.
9 *The Lord hath heard my supplication;*
the Lord will receive my prayer.
10 *Let all mine enemies be ashamed and sore vexed:*
let them return and be ashamed suddenly.

THE TODAH

The *todah* is the *musical thanksgiving* sung in the temple after the crisis is over. Examples are Psalms 18, 32, and 116. So now we have a major principle from which to work. One song (*qinah*) expresses my crisis, where I'm at, what I'm feeling. When God has brought me through the crisis, I now sing a song of thanksgiving and victory. A short example is Psalm 32 where the whole Psalm, not just a verse, is organized as a *chiasmux*, from *chiasm*, (see Chapter 7, pps 99-100 for a definition). Here's Dr. Craigie's outline:

Part I	(1) Wisdom	1-2	A
	(2) Thanksgiving	3-5	B
Part II	(1) Thanksgiving	6-8	B^1
	(2) Wisdom	9-10	A^1
Conclusion		11	

[1] Blessed is he whose transgression is forgiven,
whose sin is covered.
[2] Blessed is the man unto whom the Lord imputeth not iniquity,
and in whose spirit there is no guile.

[3] When I kept silence,
my bones waxed old through my roaring all the day long.
[4] For day and night thy hand was heavy upon me:
my moisture is turned into the drought of summer. Selah.
[5] I acknowledged my sin unto thee,
and mine iniquity have I not hid.
I said," I will confess my transgressions unto the Lord";
and thou forgavest the iniquity of my sin. Selah.

[6] For this shall every one that is godly pray unto thee
in a time when thou mayest be found:
surely in the floods of great waters they shall not come nigh unto him.
[7] Thou art my hiding place;
thou shalt preserve me from trouble;
thou shalt compass me about with songs of deliverance. Selah.
[8] I will instruct thee and teach thee in the way which thou shalt go:
I will guide thee with mine eye.

[9] Be ye not as the horse, or as the mule,
which have no understanding:
whose mouth must be held in with bit and bridle, lest they come near unto thee.
[10] Many sorrows shall be to the wicked:
but he that trusteth in the Lord, mercy shall compass him about.

[11] Be glad in the Lord, and rejoice, ye righteous:
and shout for joy, all ye that are upright in heart.

CONCLUSION

What you should observe from these past three chapters is how structured Biblical music really is. Songs come out of the experiences of life. Praise songs have various types, some of which are boisterous like the *halals*, others more reflective and thoughtful. Most all of the song lyrics have significant emotional depth. So when Paul says we can boldly approach the throne of God, here are the parameters for doing so in song.

One should also take note of the high level of writing skill contained in Biblical song lyrics. Everyone who wrote and was published in the Bible, had strong grammar skills, deploying deft use of imagery and adjectives with lots of emotion.

Considering which culture you're in as you read this book, starting with the *Song of Moses* in Deuteronomy, which of these songs with this emotional depth would be permitted to be sung in your church, today?

CHAPTER 7

BIBLICAL TECHNIQUES OF LYRIC WRITING

The purpose of this chapter is to review some of the techniques used by the Bible writers to create songs, psalms, poetry and proverbs. These techniques come out of Israelite tradition and may not work in some language groups. The source of this material comes from Dr. Ronald B. Allen's *And I Will Praise Him* and Dr. C. Hassell Bulloch's *An Introduction to the Old Testament Poetic Books*. Other insights were gleaned from Drs. Leslie C. Allen and Peter C. Craigie, authors of *Psalms 101-150* and *Psalms 1-50* in the *Word Biblical Commentary Series*.

PARALLELISM

The concept of Parallelism in Hebrew songs was first discovered in 1753 by Robert Lowth and explained to the world in his book *Lectures on the Sacred Poetry of the Hebrews*. Lowth discovered three types of parallelism: *synonymous, synthetic* and *antithetical*. To this list, scholars like Dr. Ron Allen add *climactic, emblematic* and *formal parallelism*. I'll briefly define and illustrate each with examples from Drs. Ron Allen and Bulloch's books.

SYNONYMOUS PARALLELISM

The idea of the first line is imitated and answered, and possibly expanded in the second line with a change of words.

Why do the nations conspire
and the peoples plot in vain. (Psalm 2:1, NIV)

O Lord, how many are my foes!
How many rise up against me. (Psalm 3:1, NIV)

The heavens declare the glory of God;
the skies proclaim the work of his hands. (Psalm 19:1, NIV)

Each of these lines is made up of usually two to three units. For example:

The heavens	declare	the glory of God
the skies	proclaim	the work of his hands

The lyricist's task is to now see if each of the units in the first line has a matching unit in the second line. When it does, the lines are considered complete. Continuing with our example, *heavens* has *skies, declare* has *proclaim, glory* has *work of his hands*.

However, parallelism in the Bible is often incomplete.

Psalm 24:1 is an example (NIV):

The earth	is the Lord's	and everything in it.
The world		and all who live in it.

The second line is considered incomplete because the second unit in the first line has no matching unit in the second, instead, it's implied that the world *is the Lord's* and all who live in it.

ANTITHETIC PARALLELISM

Antithetic means *contrary, unfriendly, disagreeable.* Here, the second line expresses the opposite idea of the first. A simpler word for it might be *Opposite Parallelism.* Our example is Psalm 1:6 (NIV):

For the Lord watches over the way of the righteous,
but the way of the wicked will perish.

SYNTHETIC PARALLELISM

Synthetic means *substitute.* Here, the idea of one line is developed or expanded in another line without repeating the words from the first line. Psalm 95:3 and 6 are our examples (NIV):

3 *For the Lord is the Great God the great King above all gods*
6 *Come, let us bow down in worship let us kneel before the Lord our maker*

Climactic Parallelism

Dr. Ron Allen explains that with this technique the second line uses words from the first line and fills in the concept from the first line. Our example is Psalm 96:7 (NIV):

Ascribe to the Lord, O families of nations
Ascribe to the Lord, glory and strength

Emblematic Parallelism

With this technique the second line explains a word picture or figure of speech used in the first line. Our example is Psalm 42:1 (NIV):

As the deer pants for streams of water,
so my soul pants for you, O God.

Formal Relationship

With this last technique, we see two lines that basically have no parallelism in them at all. Our examples are Psalm 119:89 and Psalm 109:1 (NIV):

[89] *Your word, O Lord, is eternal;*
it stands firm in the heavens

[1] *O God, whom I praise,*
do not remain silent.

The Chiasm

Says Dr. Bulloch, "One of the basic methods of deriving greater impact from the terms used is varying their position in the line. One such method is called *chiasm* (because when diagrammed it forms the points of the Greek 'x,' which is called *chi*)."

Our example is Proverbs 2:4 (NIV):

and if you look for it as silver
and search for it as for hidden treasure

To see the *chiasm* in the Hebrew, we have to reset the English words in Hebrew order:

If you look for it
as for hidden treasure
as silver
and search for it.

Here it is simplified:

Look (A) — silver (B)
Hidden treasure (B^1) — search (A^1)

Says Dr. Bulloch, "The variation of position in the second line highlights the great value, or wisdom, which is spoken of here, by inverting the corresponding terms."

This is how the *chiasm* was constructed in Hebrew. How we construct a *chiasm* today will be influenced by the language you're writing in. Translations don't always bring out this hidden under structure in the Hebrew. So some digging is required, along with experimenting in the language you write in to attempt to adopt these principles to create new songs.

THE ACROSTIC

The *acrostic* is a psalm or song where the first letter of each line, half verse or stanza is a letter of the Hebrew alphabet in order. The acrostic psalms are: 9-10, 25, 34, 37, 111, 112, 119, and 145. Another acrostic is the *Proverbs 31 Woman*, found in Proverbs 31:10-31. The first four chapters of the book of Lamentations also use this technique where each new chapter is its own acrostic.

PRACTICAL APPLICATION

God works through the lyric songwriting techniques of a culture.

CHAPTER 8

STANDARDS & PERFORMANCE PRACTICES: FROM THE HUT TO THE HALL, FROM SAND TO THE SANCTUARY

One of the most difficult issues in church leadership with the music ministry, is defining musical standards and performance practices for both the musical leadership, and for those who volunteer in the making and singing of music to the Lord. In approaching this, we must do so in a way with Biblical principles that work for the entire church, from huts to halls, from sand to the sanctuary.

We start with the early church, which by size would be comparable to the home church. Here, there's a distinct change in how music was administrated when compared to the Tent of Meeting. Instead of having a paid staff, it's a volunteer one.[1] Instead of having a few selected by the King and his Captains charged with prophesying through music, *all* are encouraged to pursue prophesy as a gift so that the whole church is built up. Music fits in here as a tool that builds up the body. Let's see how.

PAUL - THE "MANY DAVIDS" APPROACH

In examining all of the spiritual gift lists in the New Testament and the Pastoral Epistles, you find:

- There is no spiritual gift of music
- There is no administrative office of song leader as there was in the Temple

[1] This should not be a signal for a modern church to decide that members in the music department should be paid less than the pastoral staff, given that some apostles did take money from their local churches, but we don't know how much given the persecution of the period. With the Jerusalem church, members like Phillip were full time and were paid a *stipend*. We have no direction from the Bible as to how much this was.

Instead, we see the encouraging and developing of, "many Davids," within the congregation who support and encourage each other through:

- Bringing a work to sing at the service
- Singing to each other as David did with Saul
- Singing to God as David and other members of the Temple music staff did in their times alone with God
- Singing to themselves (thus applying musically what God commanded Joshua to do – murmuring Scripture to yourself under your breath day and night)
- Creating a work for a larger group of singers and musicians to participate in (called a *spiritual ode* by Paul)

All of these principles work easily in a smaller group situation in just about any place in the world, and even in a spacecraft if two or more Christians are onboard to form an *ekklesia*. At such a local level, leadership can be developed and growth fostered, provided the right person is leading the group or church. The advantage musically is that no one person is being Mr. or Ms. Music.

We need to make an important observation. What Paul wrote is to the whole church, big or small. The challenge in a larger church is putting this teaching to work, getting people involved and seeing what the Holy Spirit might birth and launch.

THE ONLY PASSAGES ON MUSIC & THE CHURCH

Since there are only three New Testament passages, all by Paul, that teach us about how music is to be used in the *ekklesia,* we need to look at them carefully. Two of the three passages are for corporate worship while the third is about personal worship. We'll examine each individually then pull the points together for a set of practical principles for use in the *ekklesia*.

I CORINTHIANS 14:26

How is it then, brethren? when ye come together, every one of you hath a psalm, hath a doctrine, hath a tongue, hath a revelation, hath an interpretation. Let all things be done unto edifying.

COLOSSIANS 3:16

Let the word of Christ dwell in you richly in all wisdom; teaching and admonishing one another in psalms and hymns and spiritual songs, singing with grace in your hearts to the Lord.

EPHESIANS 5:18-19

And be not drunk with wine, wherein is excess; but be filled with the Spirit; Speaking to yourselves in psalms and hymns and spiritual songs, singing and making melody in your heart to the Lord;

6 KEY ACTION PHRASES

There are six key action phrases in these three verses to guide us.

- One has a psalm
- All things be done unto edifying
- The word of Christ dwell in you richly in all wisdom
- Teaching and admonishing one another in psalms and hymns and spiritual songs
- Speaking to yourselves in psalms and hymns and spiritual songs
- Singing and making melody with grace in your heart to the Lord

ONE HAS A PSALM

When the *ekklesia* gathers, one brings a psalm. By the wording, I think it's fair to assume that at least two people in the Corinthian church played the lyre. According to the *Theological Dictionary of the New Testament*, the word *psalm,* as used in this passage to a Greek community, most likely means *a song accompanied by a plucked or strummed instrument*. It could be original. It could be a song everyone knows. Someone might sing a solo, while the whole group might sing if they know it. Today, it could be performed with either a strummed instrument or a MIDI keyboard.

Bringing a psalm, organizationally, sounds pretty loose. And it can be. Or it can be planned. It just depends on the situation. But again, this teaching is for the whole church, large or small. So the challenge in the larger church is to weave this in as part of the fabric of the service. And if several are gifted, they can be set on a rotating calendar to perform in the appropriate season. The point - when possible, don't use the same people over and over. Get folks involved.

ALL THINGS DONE FOR EDIFYING

For Paul, the key "quality" feature of a church service was that all aspects, including the music, were to edify and build up those attending. In Chapters 2 and 3, we learned what edifying means, so I won't repeat it here. Paul's point is that even music must be used to build up the *ekklesia* individually and corporately. A practical point arising from this is that when the teaching builds and the music builds up, people see value and perceive their time is being well managed. In some geographic areas, that's not a factor. But as personal communications via the Internet and other sources get down to the village level, managing people's time well will become an important factor in all cultures.

THE WORD DWELLING RICHLY AND IN WISDOM

This phrase sets up what's to come. Before we can teach and admonish one another through song, more than knowing the Word from a standpoint of memorization, it has to live in us, and be deployed with wisdom. Colossians 3:16 tells us that the word (*logos*) is to inhabit us abundantly in all wisdom (*sophia*).

In Matthew 12:42 the word *sophia* is used to describe the wisdom of Solomon.

In Matthew 13:54 it's used by people speaking of Christ, inquiring among themselves where he got such wisdom.

It's used in Proverbs 1:2 (Septuagint), *"to know **wisdom** [sophia] and **instruction** [paideia]."* [2]

TEACHING AND ADMONISHING ONE ANOTHER

Out of wisdom in dealing with each other relationally, (and this is a key word), through song we:

- **Teach -** *(didasko)* line upon line, precept upon precept
- **Admonish -** *(neutheteo)* which means gently correcting through a psalm, hymn or spiritual song (which makes sense in light of Luke 4:18-19)

[2] *Paideia* means the whole training and education of children and also, by correcting mistakes and curbing passions, instruction which aims at increasing virtue, chastisement, chastening.

Didasko is the word used to describe how Jesus taught. It means line upon line, precept upon precept, according to Greek expert Kenneth Wuest. To get an idea of what that kind of teaching looks like, study the *Sermon on The Mount* in Matthew 5-7.

The use of *neutheteo* is very interesting because nouthetic counselling is at the heart of Jay Adams' book *Competent to Counsel*. So what Paul is instructing is that we create songs that gently correct, or counsel, using different song types.

We find songs like this in the Psalms, as there are songs in The Collection that teach and that admonish. These become models for new songs, written in wisdom, selected in wisdom, and performed in wisdom.

SPEAKING TO YOURSELVES

This is an important verse because here, Paul ties music together with what the Angel of The Lord instructed Joshua to do.

- **Speaking -** *(laleo)*
- **To yourselves -** *(heautou)*. The word is first used in Joshua 1:8 in the Septuagint. If we compare to the Masoretic Text, we have *hagah*. Both mean essentially the same. So we have a match. Whether it's *hagah* in Hebrew or *heautou* in Greek, we murmur Scripture to ourselves.

Paul takes this to the next logical step by saying we sing to ourselves. Let's confirm this application by looking at the first three uses of *heautou* in Matthew.

Matthew 3:9 - the first use - is where Jesus says, *"And think not to say **within yourselves**... [heautou]"*

Matthew 9:3 - the second use - says, *"And, behold, certain of the scribes said **within themselves** [heautou], This man blasphemeth."*

Matthew 9:21 - the third use - says, *"For she said **within herself** [heautou], If I may but touch his garment, I shall be whole."*

What we have here are three methods:

1. I murmur to myself aloud by singing to myself
2. I sing silently within my mind
3. I sing to others

Paul is instructing us to do what we already do. When you learn a song you like, sometimes you sing it aloud, other times quietly to yourself. Then there are times that a song just "plays" in your mind. And then, perhaps in a home fellowship or church service, you sing it aloud to each other and to the Lord.

Paul is teaching us to do this as a matter of practice.

Singing And Making Melody In Your Heart To The Lord

We've learned about singing to ourselves and each other. Now Paul gives us important instructions on singing to the Lord.

- **Singing -** *(ado)*, means to sing.
- **Making melody -** *(psallos)*, meaning to make or play music with an instrument
- **Heart -** *(kardia)*, the center of your mind and emotions

So regardless of our playing or singing skills, we sing aloud to God playing whatever instrument we know. And it's not a mental exercise. We play from our hearts. It's heartfelt. But we do so as an outward expression of being filled with the Holy Spirit.

Observations

1. When the *ekklesia* gathers, the music performed individually or sung corporately must edify, build up
2. We sing songs that teach, line upon line, precept upon precept
3. We sing songs that lovingly correct and counsel
4. We sing to ourselves by murmuring or by playing a song in our minds
5. We sing to the Lord with grace and from our hearts, regardless of our skill level

NEW TESTAMENT SONG TYPES

The Old Testament has many song types with lyrics as you've seen. But the New Testament has but one or two lyrics. We've defined psalm. The concept of a first century hymn is lost to us but it's possible we have an example in Ephesians 5:14:

Awake thou that sleepest
And arise from the dead
And Christ shall give thee light.

We also don't know what a spiritual ode is (*pneumatikos*), but we have two possibilities.

In examining Thayer's definition of *spiritual*, it could mean the Holy Spirit singing through us. This would then explain what Paul wrote in I Corinthians 14 when he said, *"I sing with my **spirit** [pneuma] and I sing with my **mind** [nous]."*

A second option, and I think the more accurate one musically, is found in the word *ode*, which in classical Greek meant *an elegant, stately song in three parts: strophe, antistrophe, and epode*. It could also be performed with a choir. So now within the gathering of the *ekklesia* the musical imperatives are:

- Original or known works performed by individuals
- Original or known extended works performed by a group

With Paul's model, Christian music flows from the body starting with the individual and extending to longer works performed by an ensemble with a choir. Unlike the Tent of Meeting through the Temple period, it lacks a formalized structure. And given the persecution the early church faced, this would make sense.

What I like about Paul's model is that it's inclusive. You're only left out if you choose to be.

WHAT ABOUT CRAFT?

We have no direct instruction as to how proficient early Christian singer/songwriters were required to be. Practical writing experience suggests two possible approaches.

First, then, as now, there are always those who do music for fun, grow to a certain level and then stop. Second, there are those to whom God has pre-ordained a lifetime's work (*ergon*) in music. Those who sense that calling need to develop themselves accordingly. Those standards and practices we will look at in the next chapter.

MUSIC, THE MIND AND THE ARMOR OF GOD

In his book, *Rediscovering God's Church*, Derek Prince points out that putting on the armor of God, as Paul wrote about starting at Ephesians 6:10, is to protect the mind, Satan's battleground in our lives. When we sing to ourselves Scripture and appropriate song lyrics, we build ourselves by putting material in our thoughts that protects the mind.

SO LET'S SUMMARIZE:

- The *ekklesia* gathers to be built up. It can gather for other reasons, but the primary purpose is for building up those in attendance.
- Not one music person, but "many Davids"[3]
- Music is to be prophetic, to build up believers
- Music is used to teach and to gently correct
- It can be a simple work all the way up to extended works performed with choir and instruments
- We sing to ourselves and to each other
- We sing to the Lord

The principles outlined here are for any sized church, anywhere.

[3] With Paul's model of the church and how music should be used, there's no one worship leader at this time. Thus, many personnel problems churches encounter with praise band leaders and worship leaders are avoided.

Chapter 9

Music Leadership In The Large Church

When we examine the musical leadership practices set forth by David for the *ekklesia* of the Old Testament via the Tent of Meeting, we find organizational practices applicable today that have been tested and proven to work for many centuries. In a large church, the Holy Spirit certainly can, and does, lead through spontaneity. But, as first instructed to Moses from Jethro, He also works and leads in these larger, more structured situations through leadership where there are defined job descriptions and responsibilities, and a Spirit-sensitive departmental structure.

Differences Between David's Time And Paul's

Key differences between David's time with the *ekklesia*/Tent of Meeting and the *ekklesia*/home church of Paul is that music performances in the Pauline model:

- Were strictly volunteer
- Had no set performance quality standards and practices (that we're aware of through Scripture)
- Were done with volunteers, and not paid staff
- Recruited a choir as needed

With the Tent of Meeting music staff, and later the Temple, things were a little different. The purpose of music didn't change. But how it was implemented was drastically different because it was handled by Levites who were "paid staff" and were provided housing. As a result:

- Since the Levites were recipients of the tithe, including those on the music team, they were subject to scheduling, oversight and direction.
- Because they were paid staff, standards and practices *could* and *were* set and maintained.

- The position of song leader was not a training ground for new "prophets" (aka pastors) as it is in some churches today

These are three dramatic differences from David's time compared to the New Testament church. This isn't to say that you can't set standards and practices at the local level, because you can. But at the time David set these guidelines, he started with 288 Levitical musicians and singers *already* skilled and trained to sing to the Lord. By comparison to today, some churches are praying for a pianist to show up!

Here I want to make an observation. While the music of the Tent of Meeting was performed with new instruments made by David, it was largely performed on the instrument of the people, the lyre, a musical instrument that could be either strummed or plucked. Today, the instrument of the people is the acoustic guitar, followed by keyboards. The great French symphonist, Hector Berlioz, was a guitarist. And he created amazing music starting from that instrument. A church lacking a pianist can build a strong music department starting with a single guitarist. The key for such a start, is to encourage musical growth through proficiency.

Temple Leadership Positions

Under David's direction, Tent of Meeting music personnel had clear titles and job descriptions. These positions and job descriptions are still valid today, regardless of church size. The positions and job titles were:

- Song leaders (plural)
- Singers
- Ruler of the singers (who also directed choral and instrumental)
- Musicians, skilled and accomplished
- The Songwriter/Composer
- The Chief Musician

Let's look at each.

SONG LEADERS

What the Temple called song leaders, we call worship leaders. Whether the Masoretic Text or the Septuagint, the language is similar. Song leaders lead the congregation in singing to the Lord. It's this relationship aspect of singing to the Lord that we usually call worship. The song leader was put on a rotation schedule for service (I Chron. 25:8).

Let's look at I Chronicles 6:31-32 (author's expanded paraphrase):

These are the men David had stand above, with an open hand, for the service of song in the house of Jehovah after the Ark of the Covenant was put in a settled spot. They ministered in front of the residence of the tabernacle of the assembly, singing songs with musical accompaniment until Solomon built the house of Jehovah in Jerusalem. They stood in the work determined for them.

The song leaders physically stood in a position above the assembly. The Hebrew makes clear that this is an open outstretched hand, not a closed hand. In fact, the Hebrew here is the same as that used to describe the hand of God. Thus, it carries the meanings of power and direction.

There are two ways to understand this passage.

First, musical research on the Psalms done by the late Suzanne Haik-Vantoura discovered markings in the Masoretic text (and pre-Masoretic texts) requiring the use of both left and right hands to help singers and the congregation accurately sing both pitch and verbal accents. Thus, a musical reason the hand was open was to direct the congregation in singing the lyrics with the correct accents, and potentially, pitches.

Second, since in Hebrew "open hand" (*yad*) is the same word as used for *the hand of God*, it carries the symbolism of power and direction because the hand:

1. Helps direct and shape the mind and emotions of the listener by directing melodic and verbal inflection
2. Points the listener to the person being sung to

David recognized that the position of song leader is a leadership position and an appointment with great responsibility.

DUTIES PERFORMED

"They stood in the work determined for them." The function and job description were worked out ahead of time so that the music leaders were clear as to what was expected of them and what they could expect in return from those calling them.

THE SINGERS

These are the singers, heads of the fathers' houses of the Levites, dwelling in the temple chambers, free from other services because they were on duty day and night. (I Chronicles 9:33, Amplified Bible)

The nature of the work of the temple was that the singers were on call 24/7 because they were on duty day and night. Their sole responsibility was singing. This practice wasn't continued with the New Testament *ekklesia*.

RULER OF THE SINGERS

And Chenaniah, ruler of the Levites in singing, was ruler of the odes for he was discerning. (I Chronicles 15:22, Septuagint)

Looking at this passage in the Septuagint, the Greek word for ruler is *archon*. The principle we should draw from this is that, in or out of music, leadership is leadership. The word for discerning, *sunetos*, also means *prudent*. From the Septuagint, we see that Chenaniah was put in charge because he was a leader with discernment. In regard to this passage, the *Jamieson, Fausset, Brown Bible Commentary (JFB)* adds this:

[Chenaniah] was not of the six heads of the Levitical families, but a chief in consequence of his office, which required learning, without regard to birth or family.

From a job perspective, Chenaniah's skills were developed by himself. In short, he had demonstrated ability. His appointment came based on his demonstrated ability to lead and for discernment. Thus, within the church, we promote by core competencies, not connections nor academic degrees which do not certify skill.

Here's the same passage, I Chronicles 15:22, from the King James:

And Chenaniah, chief of the Levites, was for song: he instructed about the song, because he was skilful.

For the word *instructed*, Jamieson, Fausset, Brown comments, *"He directed all these bands as to the proper time when each was to strike in or change their notes; or, as some render the passage, 'He led the burdens, for he was skilled,' that is, in the custom which it was necessary to observe in the carriage of the holy things."* (Ernst Bertheau)

In the 21st Century, we would observe that Chenaniah is a capable conductor able to handle both choral and instrumental ensembles including electronic instruments.

As we examined earlier, the word *skillful*, or *wise*, in King James is *bene* in Hebrew and it's first used in Genesis 41:33, 39 to describe a quality required to be the Vizier of Egypt which was found in Joseph.

Now therefore let Pharaoh look out a man discreet and wise, and set him over the land of Egypt.

Thus, the leadership qualities found in Joseph and needed as vizier of Egypt are the same leadership qualities required in those leading and directing Christian music. Those qualities were found in Chenaniah. So, musical leadership is about being:

- Self-motivated
- Able to conduct instrumental and choral
- A leader modeled after Joseph

Here I need to point out that this role, properly executed, requires as much preparation, study time and practice as any sermon because of the amount of time needed. Conductors lead! They lead and set expectations for performers because they themselves have spent time studying the music, the text, and look to determine the most effective presentation possible for the most impacting performance possible. When electronic instruments are used, more time, not less, is spent in evaluating sounds and making sure audio connections are done properly so that the instruments function within the existing sound system.

MUSICIANS: TRAINED AND ACCOMPLISHED

All these men were under the direction of their fathers as they made music at the house of the Lord. Their responsibilities included the playing of cymbals, lyres, and harps at the house of God. Asaph, Jeduthun, and Heman reported directly to the king. They and their families were all trained in making music before the Lord, and each of them -288 in all- was an accomplished musician. The musicians were appointed to their particular term of service by means of sacred lots, without regard to whether they were young or old, teacher or student. (I Chronicles 25:6-8, NLT)

God's musicians:

1. Were given ***responsibilities*** as to which instruments they were playing
2. Were specifically ***trained*** in making music before the Lord. *Trained* in Hebrew means that they were qualified and prepared
3. Were ***accomplished***, which in Hebrew means, they were complete, and expert
4. Were expected to ***serve*** by calendared times whether young or old, teacher or student, as part of their duties

Here are some other points to consider. The fathers reported directly to the King (Asaph, Jeduthun and Heman). The sons were under the direction of their fathers. Even in music, David established lines of accountability.

What the church has in this passage are Biblical guidelines for developing and establishing performance skills in playing to the Lord. Jesus said to Peter, Andrew, James and John, *"Come now and I'll build you into fishers of men"* (Mark 1:17). What a commitment Jesus made! Building music and arts people into fishers of men includes investing in them to improve their musical skills and their skills in music technology. Paul said, *"You have many teachers, but few fathers"* (I Corinthians 4:15).

The question for the church is, "Who are the musical fathers who will build musical sons into becoming fishers of men?"

THE SONGWRITER

Using a modern musical definition, David was a singer/songwriter. By definition, a singer/songwriter is a person who both writes the song with lyrics and then performs it. David did this. His personal performances were before the Lord, but his music was performed publicly by others. In some cases it was an original lyric and song, in other cases, it was a new lyric to an existing melody (see the heading for Psalm 60).

In the heading to Psalm 61 and other Psalms, we read this:

To the Chief Musician: on stringed instruments [A Psalm] of David. (Amplified Bible)

Now in Psalm 61, David writes both melody and lyric, and sends down an arranging note to the chief musician.

From the headers of Psalms 60 and 61, we can derive some principles:

- There are some in the church who, just like David, are not part of the music department but who will write songs and submit them to the Chief Musician with arranging thoughts. In a larger gathering, this is a way that each, "brings a psalm"

- There are some in the music department who will also create new songs. This, too, is how each, "brings a psalm"

- A Christian songwriter may not be called to a full time position of songwriting. Like David, they may have other duties to attend to

- Once written, the song is taken to the Chief Musician for consideration

- The songwriter can suggest appropriate instruments for the song, but the arrangement and performance are left to the chief musician and the ruler of the singers

- It's a time-honored practice to take secular songs and create new lyrics for them. However, in our culture, copyright issues are involved and permissions must be cleared before live performance

The Chief Musician

So far, we've seen that there are skilled and discerning song leaders, musicians, singer/songwriters, and a Chief Musician. The title of chief musician would correspond to that of a staff arranger, staff composer, etc. The leadership responsibilities of the chief musician are:

- To oversee scoring (arranging/composing) and music preparation of original songs from other writers for the local *ekklesia's* musicians and singers

- To create and produce his own works (as Asaph did)

Historically, we could say that Asaph's position is the forerunner to the court composer, to the Kapellmeister, and later, to Bach, who both conducted as Chenaniah, and produced as David and Asaph.

WHAT WE LEARN FROM DAVID

First and foremost, singing and playing to the Lord corporately is serious business because you're shaping and feeding the *nephesh* (soul) of a large group of people. For some churches, that could be in the thousands per service. If the complete service is broadcast on television or over the Internet, a single service could impact, literally, millions. What David put in place was a system of checks and balances with responsibility and accountability at all levels.

Second, there is no "closed set" between the church music department and the congregation, especially if the church has a really strong praise band. "Bring a psalm" speaks to participation and inclusion, not exclusion. David as King was not directly part of the Tent of Meeting music department but he still participated.

Third, performing in service for a season is a duty and responsibility for those capable of doing so. Says the Bible, not me.

MUSICAL LEADERSHIP DEMANDS SKILL, WISDOM AND COMPETENCY

In or out of music, effective leadership defines what it wants and articulates it clearly so that people know what to do and what's expected of them. Part of being a competent musical leader is being skilled enough to hear musically what you want to accomplish and then knowing how to get people to do it. The less you know, the more you need others to help you do your job. That's not leadership.

Musical leadership must be supported by the Senior Pastor. Here's a story to explain my point. A friend of mine was choir director for a church. In the church was a flautist we'll call Florence. Florence the Flautist wanted to play in church (to do something for God), but she didn't want to practice her part. So when my friend gave her some musical correction during a rehearsal, she left in a huff, called the pastor, complained, and then the pastor "chewed out" my friend.

Was the Senior Pastor right or wrong in that decision? Whether the answer is yes or no depends on whether or not standards and practices were put in place that set the expectations of those performing and gave the conductor his boundaries for critiquing poor, unpracticed performances. Such guidelines weren't set, and as a result, the leadership of the choir director was undermined.

That said, we must practically understand that not all people participating in a church music program are there to lead others in singing to the Lord. Some are, and it distinctly shows up in their singing and playing. Others are there simply because they like to sing in a group, nothing more. When corrected, some don't hesitate to let the musical leadership know that they are doing the church a real "favor" through their musical presence.

Similar issues happen in praise bands, too, where players simply won't practice outside of church because they've "got the Spirit" and somehow feel they don't need to practice. The practices of the Tent of Meeting speak to this false belief and teaching from some musicians.

Can you imagine King David's response if a Levite musician said to him, "I don't have to practice, I've got the Spirit?" My guess is that flowers would not have been accepted for the funeral. The whole point is this: leaders must *lead*. And growing churches must set clear written guidelines of what's expected so leaders *can* lead.

If we don't do this, how are we being salt and light and impacting the world around us when we behave no differently, and in some cases worse, than non-believers?

With this I need to point out a growing anti-education trend among many church musicians and those involved with music performance and production. There seems to be this false pride about how well a person performs coupled with their inability to read music. Music notation is a language. To borrow from Paul, if we cannot "speak that way" to one another, I am a foreigner to you and you are a foreigner to me. That's a leadership principle because it involves effective communication.

Practical Considerations

As one who writes for a living, the practical applications here are self-evident, but may not be so to the local *ekklesia*. What has not been so self-evident is the need for leaders in music modeled after Joseph. God's musicians (using the term generically to encompass all we've read so far) must be both leaders and skilled in their craft. Not one or the other, but both/and.

Second, in thinking of musical proficiencies, we must be mindful of the hut-to-the-hall principle. Musical proficiencies in western music are not the proficiencies of all cultures. And this must be considered when creating job descriptions outside the industrialized nations. In the Pauline model, proficiency is up to the individual and their calling. In the Temple, craftsmanship is required.

Overall, to avoid confusion and dissent, church leadership ideally should determine, in advance of hiring a music director, the model for the music department to be used, along with the standards of performance for both paid and volunteer staff. The Pauline model of what we think of as the home church is more free, uses volunteers (non-paid staff), and is more spontaneously driven because it's smaller. The Temple model is about organization, quality standards and practices with a fully paid staff including the singers (choir) performing seasonally.

To apply these principles in a growing or larger church setting is the act of leadership.

CONSISTENT USE OF MUSIC

Even with defined roles, the purpose and use of music with the *ekklesia* is consistent. I say this because, in the Septuagint, the Israelites are also called the *ekklesia*. So whether it's at the national level or the small group level with followers of Christ, the purpose and use of music remains consistent across both Old and New Testaments.

CHAPTER 10

BASIC PERFORMANCE CONSIDERATIONS

Having looked carefully at lyric content, we must now focus on the communication of music that comes through both live and recorded performances. What follows are general principles that can be applied in any age in virtually any culture. These principles are valid from the home church to the larger church.

MELODY, HARMONY, BEAT AND RHYTHM

First in importance are lyrics, because they shape the soul. Melody, harmony, beat and rhythm support the lyric. They're totally dependent on time and place.

VOCAL CLARITY – SOLO

Words must be clearly enunciated. With Christian music, no one should ever have to guess what words are being sung. If the lyric cannot be understood clearly, especially on first listening, then more practice is required. Every word sung needs to be clearly understood. No exception.

In some pop styles, it's fashionable to improvise with a lyric especially on a sustained pitch. More often than not, this negatively impacts the lyric because attention is being drawn to the singing style rather than the lyric content. With Christian music, the focus is always on the lyric. Vocally improvise judiciously.

VOCAL CLARITY - ENSEMBLES WITH TWO OR MORE VOCALISTS

Enunciation and singing together are critical. Where voices sing in harmony, it should be practiced so that the supporting harmony doesn't draw away from the lyric. Harmony parts should always be sung slightly softer than the melody so that the lyric predominates. Phrasing needs to be worked on so that the lyric is clear.

INSTRUMENTAL DYNAMICS

Regardless of the culture, instrumentalists should play, on average, one to two dynamic levels below the vocalists. And be in tune. Otherwise, the vocalist is fighting to be heard and lyrical impact is minimized.

LIVE MIX

Again, with Christian music, clarity is king. Voices must be mixed so the words are clearly understood. If the words aren't being heard clearly, check the singer for enunciation, the monitors, and the microphones, if they're available.

Instruments need to be below the voices in volume. If the instruments drown out the lyrics, then the mix is neutralizing the song's impact.

A live mix sounds different when people are in the auditorium because the human body absorbs sound. Listen before the audience arrives, listen after the audience arrives and adjust accordingly.

THE CONDUCTOR

Chenaniah is our model. The conductor must be able to work with vocal and instrumental and, where electricity is available, with electronic instruments.

DEVELOPING YOUR CRAFT

In looking at Paul's model for the church, there are no specific requirements for developing one's craft and skill in music. At the same time, in Proverbs we're taught to buy wisdom, knowledge and understanding (see Proverbs 23:23). If you have a growing sense that part of the work you're to walk in during your time on Earth is to write and produce music in some way, develop your craft.

CONCLUSION

WORDS OF ENCOURAGEMENT & ADVICE

I want to close by giving you some thoughts that I hope you'll take to heart.

DISCOVER HOW YOU'RE FEARFULLY AND WONDERFULLY MADE.

One of the biggest problems I find with most Christians, especially in the arts, is that, unlike David in Psalm 139:14, they don't know how they're fearfully and wonderfully made. Finding that out will make all the difference in your life and your perspective. You can begin finding out by reading a few books and taking some self-tests to help you better understand how God designed you.

Now Discover Your Strengths - Published by Gallup and based on interviews and tests with over 1 million managers. Read the book and take the online test. You'll get back a test score showing your top five strengths.

Please Understand Me - It's an awful title but a great book. Written by David Keirsey and Marilyn Bates, you'll take a temperaments test showing you your four-letter code which is a key to understanding your temperament. But that's only the beginning, because the next book is...

Do What You Are - Modeled after Keirsey-Bates. After analyzing the test scores of tens of thousands of respondents, the authors created a book that lets you look up your score and see what job occupations your temperament has had the most success in.

After going through these three books, here's what you'll learn – that God did not make a mistake when He created you and that you're designed for success. You're designed to be a *winner*, not a whiner. There's a race for you to run and finish. Too often, the negative way we think about ourselves interferes with the work we're called to walk in. I find this especially true of artists who by nature are more self-critical. So, consider these words of Samuel to King Saul from the New Living Translation.

And Samuel told him, "Although you may think little of yourself, are you not the leader of the tribes of Israel? The LORD has anointed you king of Israel. (I Samuel 15:17, NLT)

Our focus needs to be on what God has called us to do, not on how little we think of ourselves. You may have issues and struggles to work through. You may have poor self-esteem because of the past. Nonetheless, this is your time. Run the race and finish it.

With this, I'd encourage you to get a second, simpler book on temperaments called *The Two Sides of Love* by Gary Smalley along with *The Five Love Languages* by Gary Chapman.

Finally, I'd encourage you to talk with your local pastor about a spiritual gifts test to discover your place in the *ekklesia*.

READ! ESPECIALLY FICTION

Some will disagree with this. But song lyrics come from words. You won't learn your craft playing games or watching videos and TV. Reading fiction helps you develop coloristic words and phrases. Keep a notebook. When you find a color phrase, underline it in the book and then write it in your notebook. Looking at various translations, apply this to your study of the Psalms.

For English speaking songwriters, ideally, you should have a working vocabulary level up to the 7th grade which is the grade level at which newsweekly magazines are written. Your own personal library should include the *Rodale Synonym Finder*, along with several dictionaries and a rhyming dictionary.

DEVELOP YOUR CRAFT - PRACTICE

Musicians on the Tent of Meeting music staff were skilled in playing to the Lord. The same consideration applies to songwriters, musicians, song leaders, and composers.

Imitate How David Was Vulnerable In Song

Today there's this prevalent idea that being "honest" is saying whatever comes to your mind. You can write an honest lyric without laying out all the garbage. The following Psalms by David were based on specific events in his life. Read the event in Scripture then the psalm to see how David made himself vulnerable through his music: 3, 7, 18, 30, 34, 51, 52, 54, 56, 57, 59, 60 and 63.

Listen To A Lot Of Music And Develop Your Sound

What's musically hot today is gone tomorrow. I hear way too many songs that sound like everyone is trying to "sound like" someone else. To use a band expression, you're not here to do "cover songs" for Jesus by imitating everyone else. If you write in someone else's style, who are *you*?

It's OK If You Do Music Part Time. David Did

Some will be called to do music part time, like David; others full time, like Asaph. Even as a "part-timer" David's lyrics set the standard. Start where you are, but choose to maintain high standards of excellence.

Don't Put Your Song On A Par With Scripture

This is a problem that pervades Christian music. Some feel that after they've created a song it shouldn't be touched. The harmony shouldn't be modified. The lyric shouldn't be revised. The melody shouldn't be changed. All of this because, "the Lord gave it to them." I don't know where this teaching came from but this is wrong theology. There is no teaching, not even from Paul, that suggests that what you create on the first draft is "it."

Now, you might get blessed and occasionally write a song that's so strong it's already finished with no further revision necessary. But unless you have to create in a hurry like film/TV professionals do, that's rare.

I know of two Christian songwriters who came out of well known acts during the Jesus movement days. One can write several different songs in a day and they all sound different. The other has song lyrics with a strong prophetic message. Like

Oscar Hammerstein II and Alan Jay Lerner, she can take up to six weeks to complete a lyric.

Amateurs will strongly disagree, but consider whatever you get your first draft. When it's finished, come back and play it again. The professional will always hear where it needs work, and where it doesn't. But the professional always seems to know when it's done. Moreso the Spirit-empowered professional.

Copyright Your Material And Get It Registered

When the Bible was written, there were no copyrights. Today we have copyrights. Copyright your song with the appropriate agency in your country's government. Once the song is written and registered, even with Christian music, you have the beginnings of a literary estate. The copyrighted song is a financial instrument carrying numerous rights for licensing. The entire Temple staff was salaried (as Levites they received a portion of the tithes). As a royal priesthood of believers (the new Levites), we're not on staff. So if God wants to provide for you through your music, don't shut the door. Do the work and register the songs. Given the tenor of the times and the Internet, you may need to promote them by sending out MP3s, etc.

Watch carefully the Internet sites where you post your music because some Internet site agreements state that once you've posted a work, the site shares in the copyright and anyone on the site can take your work and do what they want with it, license free.

According to various sources, monthly, 1 billion songs are downloaded illegally. In short, be wise.

What If...

What if you're in a local church, you're a song/music creator, and the door, for whatever reason, is closed to having your songs performed locally? Rather than list the many reasons why this might happen, I offer this advice:

- Keep writing and playing to the Lord. Don't cut off that part of your relationship with the Lord through music.
- Find someone who can check the theological integrity of your lyrics.

- Copyright your work.
- Record your work and create MP3s of it.
- Start a web site and post your music on it. The Internet is a global communication medium and through it you can create songs to sing to one another.

APPENDIX I

WISDOM'S ROLE

A concept rarely taught in the Christian arts is that those whom God appoints as His artists, He also bestows with a special wisdom. The Hebrew word for wisdom is *chokmah* and it's the same word used in Proverbs that Solomon tells us we are to pursue. In the Septuagint and the Greek New Testament, the word is *sophia.*

Throughout Job, Proverbs and Ecclesiastes, *chokmah* is translated *wisdom.* But in Exodus, it's most often translated as *skill.* To see this in action, here are three passages I've paraphrased inserting the word *chokmah* into the text.

The Lord also said to Moses, "Look, I've selected Uri's son Bezalel, Hur's grandson from the tribe of Judah. I've filled him with the Spirit of God in ***chokmah****, giving him wisdom, intelligence and skill in all kinds of crafts."* (Ex. 31:1-3, Author's paraphrase)

In the Septuagint, intelligence is rendered as *sunesis,* which means *a flowing together of knowledge.* Skill is from the Hebrew *da'ath* which also means *cunning.*

"Bezelel has my ***chokmah*** *in both cutting and setting gems and with wood. He's a master at every craft."* (Ex. 36:6, Author's paraphrase)

And Moses reported, "The Lord has selected Uri's son Bezalel, Hur's grandson of the tribe of Judah. The Lord has filled Bezalel with his Spirit, given him ***chokmah****, intelligence and skill in all types of crafts."* (Ex. 35:30-31, Author's paraphrase)

The Lord has given them ***chokmah*** *as jewelers, designers, weavers, and embroiderers...* (Ex 35:35 Author's paraphrase)

Bezalel, Oholiab, and the other craftsmen, to whom the Lord has given ***chokmah****, skill, and intelligence, will build and furnish the Tent of Meeting, just as God commanded.* (Ex 36:1, Author's paraphrase)

What is wisdom/skill in music? First, it's a special empowering of the Holy Spirit. Second, from the word *sophia* (as defined by Strong's New Testament Greek Lexicon), we understand that broadly, it means broad and full of intelligence; used of the knowledge of very diverse matters, always giving the sagest advice, skill in the management of affairs devout and proper prudence in communication with men not disciples of Christ, skill and discretion in imparting Christian truth, the wisdom of God as evinced in forming and executing counsels in the formation and government of the world and the scriptures.

From ***sunesis***, an ability to put it all together.

From ***da'ath***, making things work in a cunning, step-above way.

This is empowered skill and leadership which, in Pentecostal circles, is called *anointed*.

A person called by God to an artistic purpose, empowered by the Holy Spirit, will demonstrate this special unction. Even at the very beginning, you'll see a hint of it. The more consistent hands-on work the Christian artist does, the more it appears.

APPENDIX II

PICKING MUSIC FOR THE WESTERN CHURCH SERVICE

After reading the chapter *Selecting Your Music* in Rick Warren's *The Purpose Driven Church*, and comments by David Murrow in *Why Men Hate Going to Church*, I woke up one morning sensing I needed to discuss what music should be selected, and what should songwriters/composers be asked to create.

Based on Acts 17:26, my view is that the first answer should not be stylistic. In the mid '90s when *The Purpose Driven Church* was written, we had roughly 40 different lifestyles as defined by the PRIZM system. So defining contemporary rock was a little easier. Now in 2007, we're up to 80! Now defining contemporary rock is more difficult because there are more music styles. With this I see three broad groups:

- **The Churched -** those currently attending a local church
- **The New Unchurched -** follow Christ but who stay home for a variety of reasons and some of whom support TV ministries
- **The Unchurched -** don't follow Christ, rarely go to church if ever

RE: THE NEW UNCHURCHED

The term *New Unchurched* is my own and describes a growing population of Followers not connected locally for a variety of reasons. Two key factors about the New Unchurched are that either they can't physically get to the church, or they're "turned off" and decide not to go. Jesus commanded *"Go teach learners..."* but too often the message from the local church is, "Y'all come down." This pattern, which is prevalent from Los Angeles to London, drives some Christians into some form of alternative gathering of the *ekklesia*, most often, Christian TV, which is a gathering with no human contact and *koinonia* (fellowship).

One challenge for the church in the 21st Century and beyond is in learning how to integrate media and the Internet to help people stay connected with a local body. And with that comes strategically using music, whose purpose is to edify.

4 Broad Groups Of The New Unchurched

While there are others, here are what I believe to be the dominant four:

- Men in general
- Commuters
- Disabled
- Single parent

Men

A full discussion of this group is beyond the scope of this book. But I want to give you some reading references to consider: *Revolution* by George Barna, *Why Men Hate Going to Church* by David Murrow and *Anointed for Business* by Ed Silvoso. It takes all three titles to explain why men are so disengaged from church. And of these, only *Why Men Hate Going to Church* covers the negative impact some worship songs have on men.

Commuters

Where we live and where we work aren't always in the same place. Too often the church forgets that there are gang and drug problems in public schools. Parents will often move their families to suburban and exurban areas where there are stable neighborhoods with quality schools, and then commute 45 minutes or more to work - one way. That's 1.5 hours sitting in a car or taking some kind of alternative transportation to get to and from work. By the time men and women get home at night, they're physically tired, not unfaithful.

The Disabled

This group is on the rise as both Pre- and Post-War Baby Boomers, and their parents, The Greatest Generation, age.

To attend church, disabled people need easy access with clearly labeled handicapped parking, an elevator, and handicapped restrooms with unwaxed floors. And there's something else that's needed: parents who will keep young ones from running around. When people fear falling, they won't come. They can't. If someone falls and hurts themselves at church, everyone is sorry the accident took place, but who comes to visit and take care of the individual who hurt themselves?

Within the music department, I've seen bizarre guidelines that keep disabled people out. One church I know of wouldn't allow disabled people in the choir because they couldn't stand up.

In the service, congregational standing for long periods of time during singing, needs to be de-emphasized. Elderly people, in particular, can't focus on singing to the Lord when they're standing in pain.

There's also the discourtesy of standing over people in wheelchairs causing them to lean back and trying to talk at an angle. This is fatiguing. It only takes a second to draw up a chair or sit down in the pew to talk at eye level.

Then I see two theological issues which discourage the disabled from attending church. One is from the charismatic/Pentecostal community who will say to someone with an obvious physical issue, "If you had more faith, God would heal you." No matter how well intentioned, such comments hurt people and discourage weekly attendance because it makes them feel like spiritual failures.

The flip side of that are those denominations who, instead of praying with faith for healing, will pray, "Lord, if it's your will..." Instead of inspiring and boosting faith, either position is a discourager. Another consideration is that, depending on the severity of the injury or disability, specialized transportation may be required for which the disabled person must pay for "out of pocket." In some areas, such paid transportation can cost $100-$200 round trip. Some areas provide free transportation for the disabled but pickup and return times are not always guaranteed.

In our area of Virginia, a recent study found that there were 4500 disabled individuals. One can only imagine how many are unchurched by default. The question the church must answer is, "are the disabled who cannot attend a weekly service lost sheep or simply discarded?"

With such issues before us, how great the need for the gift of Shepherd in the local *ekklesia*.

SINGLE PARENTS

Most of the time single parents means the divorced. I've seen too many times that the single parent/divorced are another unwanted group in some local churches. When they can't turn to God through the church, what message about our Lord do we send as we sing our hymns and praise songs?

CONTENT, NOT STYLE

When we really look at our music choices in light of these population groups, I suggest seven categories of songs by lyric content a church needs to have available to edify, regardless of music style:

- Songs that openly praise God and testify to His work in our everyday lives
- Scripture set to music
- Prophetic songs that teach, warn, counsel and encourage
- Music of encouragement
- Joyful music
- Songs of reflection
- Songs that let me know God is with me

RE: STYLE

From an arranging perspective, I have a problem with the phrase "contemporary rock." My concern is that it might be interpreted as meaning primarily *white music*, which leaves out many styles that use a rock feel of some type, and may even use modal harmony. In light of Acts 17:26, if the focus is going to be on just doing contemporary rock music, then you need to clearly define what styles that includes.

Contemporary rock, in fact any rock style, and just about any country style, is based on a dance rhythm where beats 2 and 4 are emphasized by the drummer on the snare drum and beats 1 and 3 by the bass player working with the drummer and his bass drum. Excluding blues and certain types of folk music that are triplet based, almost any musical style fits or can be adapted to fit that pattern. Even rap and hip hop work within that rhythmic pattern.

Following Paul's instruction to *"bring a psalm"*, what if someone is gifted in writing rap, or heavy metal, or Korean, or salsa? Is the church going to use them, or are they going to be "bench warmers." And if you're using the "many Davids" approach, what style is the Holy Spirit writing through these individuals?

One potential option is having specific types of music for specific services that reach specific groups as some churches are now trying.

Another way to pick music is through instrumental choices. This is more Biblical than you may realize.

We have a clue about this that runs all the way from the Tent of Meeting to Paul. The clue is using the instrument(s) of the people. From David to Paul and beyond, that instrument was the stringed lyre. Today, the instrument of the people is the guitar, followed by the piano.

The next people's instrument is the human voice.

Music was performed in the *ekklesia* for a millennia or more with one or more voices singing along with one or more acoustic instruments while the congregation gave focused attention as they listened and corporately sang to the Lord.

So, I would consider selecting some music using a solo instrument with a solo voice.

With this, you should also consider the Pastor's style of preaching and delivery. How should music support the way he brings the message to the congregation?

But in the end, I think you always need to come back to Acts 17:26. Who's there? What musical style works best for those people? If you're in a multilingual area, your church may need some specialized ethnic services. So again, Acts 17:26 comes into play. What music works best for what group?

MIDI

As the author of *How MIDI Works*, I agree with what Rick Warren said in *The Purpose Driven Church* about MIDI keyboards. As the publisher of over 200 works on MIDI keyboards, I can tell you by experience they have an amazing potential that's untapped by many churches.

Two or more keyboardists using professional MIDI keyboards can create amazing sounds, especially when combined with the standard rock rhythm section and singers. Horn and woodwind players are not left out when you realize that there are both electronic wind and brass instruments that can be connected to a MIDI keyboard. There's also the Zeta MIDI string instruments and Roland MIDI guitar controllers.

The next level is to use sample libraries on a portable laptop that keyboards and other MIDI controllers can connect to. These new sample libraries and virtual instruments provide amazing opportunities for rich, fresh, colorful musical arrangements that impact the congregation and support the pastor's message.

WHO IS THE SERVICE FOR?

You've learned from this book how music is to be used in the gathering of the *ekklesia, the called out ones* and with Christians as individuals. This brings up the practical question, *who is the service for?* Christians only, with the occasional guest; or a seeker approach for both Followers and non-Followers?

If the service is for both, then special care must be made to insure that song lyrics make sense whether the listener is a Follower or not. This does not mean, by any stretch, that lyrics should be watered down so as to appeal to a wider audience. Again, pick most any Psalm at random and read it aloud in a modern translation. The content is crystal clear. And nothing is watered down.

SERMON STYLES AND MUSIC

There are two different types of sermons, topical/series and going through a book of the Bible. Rick Warren, in *The Purpose Driven Church*, favors topical/series and explains why. Chuck Smith, founder of the Calvary Chapel movement favors going through a whole book.

We need to consider each because each has its own set of musical imperatives.

TOPICAL SERMONS OR SERMONS IN A SERIES

Since Rick Warren has written about this approach in *The Purpose Driven Church*, I refer you to that book so you can learn from Mr. Warren directly. With this style, I've sat under two approaches. One approach is topical that's still a complete study from a book of the Bible. Another is a series on a specific subject. For example, a pastor might do a series on marriage, the Holy Spirit, etc.

From a music creation perspective, if you're doing a series, then you really need to get with the pastor and get his outline early so you can either select appropriate music or create appropriate music that supports the pastor's sermons. And then, check the lyrics.

Through A Book

The years my wife Caroline and I spent at a Calvary Chapel in Southern California were some of the happiest in our lives. One summer, the Senior Pastor asked several of us to work with him in researching and preparing sermon notes for a book of the Bible. This was a great opportunity for me because I learned first hand Chuck Smith's (the founder of the Calvary Chapel movement) view on preaching. The reason Chuck Smith favors going through a book of the Bible over topical sermons is that the pastor preaching is as equally confronted as his congregation by the text and so must deal with issues as they appear in Scripture.

In our pastor's teaching, he taught as the Holy Spirit led him to prepare a message for that week. But it wasn't done in a heavy, exegetical approach where you'd spend five years in a single book! It was done in such a way that it was a joy. And in a quiet way, it also taught the congregation how to study the Word.

The great thing about such an approach musically, is that you can create many songs either direct from Scripture or based on Scripture. As a result, a unique Bible songbook can emerge.

Music Separate From The Sermon

There's another option that happens quite frequently which is to prepare music independent of the sermon in an effort to establish a worship mood. Clearly this happens all the time. But if a pastor can find someone mature enough to write music consistently that supports his sermons, I feel that the congregation is better served because the learning impact is heightened.

In advertising, I worked for years as a marketing/media planner before going back to music full time. A very famous study on ad exposure was done by Dr. Herbert Krugman of the General Electric company called *Why Three Exposures May Be Enough*. His point was that advertising was a learning affair in that a person needed to see an ad an average of three times before they learned/remembered it.

Learning from GE, if the message is backed with supporting music, the congregation will learn more. If the song is repeated and taught to the congregation, then those who remember the song can sing it to themselves (*hagah*). To use a military term, such a coordinated effort can become a force multiplier and greatly enhance the teaching impact of the pastor.

But it takes a team effort.

SONGS NOT TO PICK

We have one instruction on this from Proverbs 20:25 (NLT):

Singing cheerful songs to a person whose heart is heavy is as bad as stealing someone's jacket in cold weather or rubbing salt into a wound.

In small group situations, regardless of the group's intent, whether it's a home group, or a type of Christian 12-Step or support group, you have to be careful of the songs you sing. The wrong songs can create problems. Opening up in a group takes real courage. People who've come from deeply hurt backgrounds who open up and share have really made themselves vulnerable and any number of feelings might arise. In such moments, it may be better to simply not sing, rather than forcing people to sing something that wounds them even more deeply.

THE FINAL QUESTION

We can debate these points until the Second Coming takes place! But we have a Biblical directive to consider for each service. Regardless of style, do the lyrics of all the songs edify the *ekklesia*?

If we haven't done that, we've failed.

Resources

Used In Preparing This Book

Music Books

And I Will Praise Him: A Guide to Worship in the Psalms by Ronald B. Allen
The Craft of Lyric Writing by Sheila Davis
Ministry and Musicians by Dr. William Hooper
Jewish Music: Its Historical Development by Abraham Z. Idelsohn
David's Harp by Alfred Sendry
The Music of the Bible Revealed: The Deciphering of a Millenary Notation by Suzanne Haik-Vantoura (Author), John Wheeler (Editor), Dennis Weber (Translator)
An Introduction to the Old Testament Poetic Books by C. Hassell Bulloch

Christian Living Books

Why Men Hate Going to Church by David Murrow
Rediscovering God's Church by Derek Prince
Anointed For Business by Ed Silvoso
The Purpose Driven Church by Rick Warren
They Like Jesus But Not the Church by Dan Kimball

Commentaries & Word Studies

I Corinthians by Charles Hodge
I Corinthians by Leon Morris
Exposition of the First Epistle to the Corinthians (New Testament Commentary) by Simon J. Kistemaker
The Psalms by James Montgomery Boice
Ephesians by James Montgomery Boice
A Treasury of David by Charles H. Spurgeon

Psalms 1-50 by Peter C. Craigie (Word Commentary Series)
Psalms 101-150 by Leslie C. Allen (Word Commentary Series)
Song of Solomon - Barnes Notes on the Old Testament
The Song of Songs: Love Lyrics from the Bible by Marcia Falk
Theological Dictionary of The New Testament by Kittel
Thayer's Greek Dictionary
The New Wilson's Old Testament Word Studies
Word Studies in the Greek New Testament (4 volume set) by Kenneth S. Wuest
The Bible Knowledge Commentary by Dr. John F. Walvoord and Roy B. Zuck

STUDY BIBLES

The Tanakh (Jewish Publication Society)
The Companion Bible (Bullinger)
Thomas Nelson NKJV Study Bible
The New Living Translation Praise and Worship Study Bible
The New International Version Study Bible
The New English Translation (www.bible.org)
The Amplified Bible
The Holman Christian Standard Bible
The Apostolic Bible Polyglot - Septuagint (http://septuagint-interlinear-greek-bible.com/)
The Interlinear Bible (Hebrew and Greek) edited by Jay P. Green

ONLINE RESOURCES

The Apostolic Bible Polyglot - Septuagint
http://septuagint-interlinear-greek-bible.com/

Bible Study Tools
www.crosswalk.com
www.e-sword.net

Bayless Conley: The Holy Spirit Series - 6 Messages
http://www.answersbc.org/abcstore/display.php?cat=29&zid=1&lid=1&cartid=2007080
24682348

The Continuing Work of Suzanne Haik-Vantoura
http://www.rakkav.com/kdhinc/index2.htm

Song of Songs
http://www.rakkav.com/song/pages/song01.htm

ABOUT

PETER LAWRENCE ALEXANDER

Peter is a graduate of both the Richard Bland College of the College of William and Mary, and Berklee College of Music where he earned a Bachelor of Science Degree in Music Composition. At Richard Bland College he launched the Jazz Workshop Program which was endorsed by the late Stan Kenton. While at Berklee, he toured New England with his 20-piece Christian Big Band, performed locally with the Peter Alexander Trio, and conducted local jingle sessions.

He spent nearly a decade in advertising and marketing where part of his work as a marketing/media planner was studying how people used music. His research with radio ratings diaries ultimately laid the foundation for radio and TV profiling down to the zip code level. In the '80s, he conducted a zip code study of the members of three different Christian record clubs and discovered that, true to church growth research conducted by Dr. Donald McGavran of the Fuller School of World Missions, the geographic impact of the Holy Spirit bringing others to Christ is discernible.

In Los Angeles, he continued his studies in music by studying orchestration with the noted Hollywood orchestrator, Dr. Albert Harris, whose composition for guitarist Andres Segovia was nominated for a Pulitzer Prize, and with Arthur Morton, orchestrator for film composer Jerry Goldsmith. He also launched Alexander Publishing, which is an educational publishing house focusing on Music, Music Technology, Christian training, Christian historical fiction, the licensing of original orchestral works and Christian-themed one-person shows.

Peter worked for three years as the music tech for songwriter/composer Henry Mancini (*Pink Panther* theme, *Moon River*, and others), and understudied with film composer Jerry Goldsmith (*Secret of NIMH, Chain Reaction, Star Trek: The Next Generation*, and others).

His experiences on the scoring stages of Los Angeles enabled Peter to coordinate the beta test teams for the Vienna Symphonic Library *First Edition* and *Pro Editions*.

He recently co-produced *The Modern Symphonic Orchestra* for E-MU Systems, a division of Creative Labs, makers of the famous SoundBlaster audio cards.

Music books he's written include *How MIDI Works*, the multi-volume *Professional Orchestration Series, Applied Professional Harmony, Counterpoint by Fux, How Ravel Orchestrated: Mother Goose Suite*, and many others. Several of his books on musical instruction in orchestration and harmony have been endorsed by winners of the Academy®, Grammy®, and Emmy® Awards.

Christian titles include: *The Prayer That Gets Results, Writing and Performing Christian Music*, and *The Business Parables*.

For audio books, he's directed Emmy Award winning David Warner in *Gift of The Magi* and *The First Christmas*, and Kathy Grable in his original historical fiction work, *The Unfaithful Wife: The Story of Hosea and Gomer*. He's currently producing and scoring for audio his original treatment of *The Story of The Good Samaritan*.

His orchestral works and orchestrations include *Journey to the Third Heaven* for orchestra and choir, *Jimbo's Lullaby*, and *The Little Shepherd Boy*.

Christian songs include his setting of the *23rd Psalm, Hear O Israel The Lord Our God is One, I Call Your Name in The Night*, and *Let Him Kiss Me* from *Song of Solomon*.

Because of his expertise in music technology, Mr. Alexander writes the *Music Technology & You* column for *Film Music Weekly* published out of Los Angeles.

Peter Alexander is a polio survivor having missed the polio vaccine by nearly five years. In his youth, Peter overcame the effects of polio well enough to letter in sports, play drums, and with the encouragement of original Mercury astronaut Scott Carpenter, pursue his dream of going to the Air Force Academy and ultimately NASA. But this was not to be. With a family tradition of military service extending back to the French and Indian War, Peter made a second effort to pursue his dream of becoming a professional military officer by preparing to earn his Green Beret through the National Guard. But God said *no* again. From that point forward, he pursued the mission in music and publishing God had set for his life.

In his mid-Forties, Peter came down with post-polio syndrome, a condition in which polio comes back in later life. He completely lost his ability to hold a pencil to write music and to play keyboards. This ended his career as an orchestrator and film composer in Los Angeles.

Through prayer and healing, Mr. Alexander has been restored to the place he can now work nearly a full day, play keyboards and score with pencil. He is no stranger to the dark night of which St. Paul wrote about.

He now lives in Virginia with his wife Caroline where he continues to improve while writing and producing new works, including the recent launch of Alexander University online classes which train students literally the world over.

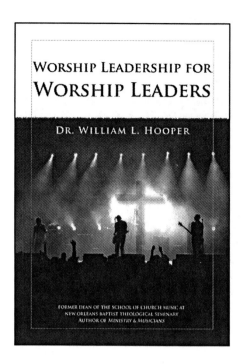

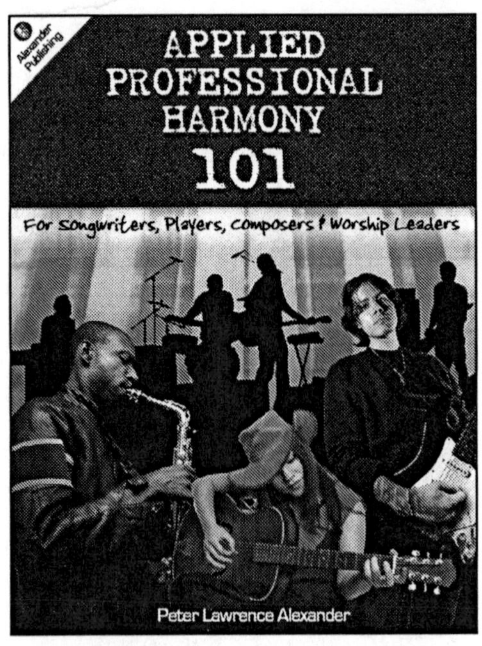

APPLIED PROFESSIONAL HARMONY 101

Peter Lawrence Alexander

Applied Professional Harmony 101 is a songwriter and composer's approach to learning harmony. Unlike traditional music courses, you're constantly writing music as you go along. By the end of APH 101 you will have learned how to create a basic demo arrangement of your song. We encourage you to use a MIDI keyboard to get the most out of your work.

"Peter Alexander in his series, Applied Professional Harmony, has created what I feel will be standard text in schools for many years to come. In a thoroughly readable style, he has managed the neat trick of erasing the lines between so called 'popular' music and 'classical' music. Read and Learn."

Henry Mancini

"If I had these books when I was in college, I'd have stayed in music school."

John Tesh

ISBN: 978-0-939067-88-6

Available from **www.alexanderpublishing.com** or through your local book store.

HOW RAVEL ORCHESTRATED: MOTHER GOOSE SUITE

Peter Lawrence Alexander

All I can say is fantastic! My students, and I were completely enthralled by the analysis you provided, as well as the score with the included piano part. Two of the students are jazz majors and were very excited about how Ravel was approaching harmonization from a chord/scale jazz harmony perspective. They really started to make a connection with Ravel's approach and what they have been learning in arranging class for big band; especially the jazz harmonization and line writing aspect of the score.

The piano part at the bottom of the score is a great teaching tool for orchestration students. All of my students stated that they would like to see more scores presented in this format. They all felt that they were gaining a better understanding on how Ravel approached orchestrating this movement because of the piano part that was included in the score.

The next time I teach my orchestration class, this will be required reading for all of my students, it is that good. I love the new approach.

Dr. Rik Pfenninger
Plymouth State University

ISBN: 978-0-939067-12-1

Printed in the United States
89805LV00003B/436-483/A

9 780939 067770